Transsexual Workers

Transsexual Workers

An Employer's Guide

Janis Walworth, MS

Center for Gender Sanity
Bellingham, Washington

Transsexual Workers: An Employer's Guide

Printed in the United States of America

 Please address inquiries to Center for Gender Sanity, PO Box 30313, Bellingham, WA 98228 or director@gendersanity.com.

ISBN 0-9665488-2-5

Photo credits: Cover photographs by Michele Kämmerer except that of herself, which is by David L. Paquin.

Contents

On the Cover

Three transsexual professionals: Michele Kämmerer, fire captain (left); Jamison Green, writer (center); Rachel Rose, home health aide (right).

Acknowledgments

This book owes its existence to the many transsexual women and men who have opened their hearts to me, shared their stories with me, challenged my assumptions and biases, and accepted me into their community. Without them I would have had neither the courage nor the inspiration to undertake this project. I feel extraordinarily fortunate to have many transsexual friends; they have enriched my life immeasurably.

It would be impossible to list all the friends, colleagues, mentors, and clients—both transsexual and non-transsexual—who helped bring this book into being. I owe thanks especially to those who read the many drafts of this book and offered their critiques and advice, especially Amy, Chris, Doug, Jeff, Jenne, Lisa, Marie, Michele, and Vivian. Their suggestions contributed much to the completeness and clarity of this book.

Finally, I am extremely grateful to my partner, Michele Kämmerer, whose financial support made it possible for me to spend the time this project required and to finally get it into print. Her unwavering belief in my ability has sustained me throughout my work.

In Brief

T*ranssexualism* is a condition in which a person's sense of identity as a woman or a man does not correspond with their genitalia and other physical sexual characteristics. Its cause is currently unknown, although there are indications that both biology and early childhood environment are factors. For male-to-female transsexuals, treatment consists of the assumption of a woman's social role, along with physical changes brought about by hormones, hair removal, and/or surgery that make the body more typically female. This process, best accomplished with the help of a psychotherapist, is called *transition.* For female-to-male transsexuals, who exist in approximately equal numbers as male-to-female transsexuals, transition is similar but in the opposite direction. Many transsexuals ultimately decide not to have genital surgery but live permanently in the role of the other sex.

Holding a job in his or her new role is an important part of the *real-life experience* or *real-life test,* a period of a year or more during which the transsexual has an opportunity to experience living in the other gender role before making a final decision about whether to have sex reassignment surgery. Although this time can be challenging for managers and coworkers, as well as the transsexual individual, many transsexuals have completed transitions smoothly in a wide variety of occupations. Their experience, which provides the basis for this book, offers valuable guidance on how best to handle the many sensitive situations that can arise.

Decisions often must be made about whether to transfer the transsexual employee to a different location within the company, whether to change her or his job responsibilities, and how to handle her or his contacts with the public. Many practical workplace matters must be resolved. The question of which restroom the transsexual employee should use often becomes a major stumbling block in a company's ability to cope with a transitioning employee; yet there are several simple solutions to this issue that are effective in most workplaces. These issues, which require multifaceted examination, are addressed in this book.

Although transsexuals have few protections against discrimination under the current laws, there are federal, state, and local statutes that have supported equal treatment of transsexuals, and more nondiscrimination laws that include gender identity are being enacted every year. Making employment-related decisions about a transsexual employee based on his or her performance record and ability to do the job, rather than on his or her transgendered status, is a prudent and fair course of action. Ensuring that a transsexual employee is treated with the same respect accorded other employees helps organizations to safeguard against legal problems.

Helping coworkers adjust to the transsexual worker's changing role is the most critical task for management. Offering or requiring diversity training or an informational meeting is helpful in most work situations. Management can help coworkers understand how they are expected to behave by making a clear statement supporting the right of transsexual employees to make decisions about their sex and gender, affirming the value of diversity in the workplace, and emphasizing a commitment to having a workplace where all employees are valued and respected. These statements should be reinforced by demonstrating appropriate ways of interacting with the transsexual employee in her or his new gender role and enacting sanctions against those who harass or intimidate the employee.

When an employer and a transsexual employee can discuss the employee's transition in advance and agree on the steps to be taken and their timing, transition usually proceeds without incident. The employee is able to take the necessary steps toward self-fulfillment, while remaining at a job where he or she is competent and valued. The employer retains the expertise of the employee, saves the expense of hiring and training a replacement, and may find the employee to be more productive and easier for others to collaborate with as he or she becomes a more whole, congruent, and authentic person. This guide, human resources specialists, unions, professional associations, gay/lesbian/bisexual employee support groups, and outside consultants can all be helpful in this process.

1 About Transsexualism: The Basics

Transsexualism is a condition in which a person's sense of identity as a man or a woman does not correspond with their genitalia and other anatomic sexual characteristics. In other words, a person who is biologically male may feel like a woman; a person who has a female body may have a sense of "really" being a man. Transsexuals are not delusional; they are aware of their actual biological sex. However, those body characteristics that signify their sex—genitalia as well as breasts, beard, voice, etc.—feel wrong to them. It seems that these parts don't belong and that they misrepresent who the person really is. This discomfort with their biological sex leads transsexuals to alter their bodies to make them more congruent with their inner identity.

Male-to-female transsexuals, or *transsexual women,* begin life as males and later identify as women and take steps to feminize their anatomy. *Female-to-male* transsexuals, or *transsexual men,* change their sex in the other direction. It is thought that there are approximately equal numbers of female-to-male and male-to-female transsexuals. Before having sex reassignment surgery, transsexuals are referred to as *preoperative,* or *preop,* whereas after completing one or more surgeries, they are *postoperative,* or *postop.*

How does a person know that he or she is a transsexual?

Transsexualism is not a condition that develops suddenly. Most transsexuals report that they felt "different" even as young children, although they may not have known exactly what that difference was. Commonly, male-to-female transsexuals say they felt that they were girls or should have been girls from as long ago as they can remember. As children, they may have preferred playing with girls and enjoyed games typically engaged in by girls, such as dolls, dress-up, and playing house. Many female-to-male transsexuals identified as boys from an early age and preferred noisier and more active play. They may have been seen as tomboys by their parents and teachers. Of course, not all children who engage in games typically played by the other sex turn out to be transsexual, and many children who later identify as transsexual behave no differently than other children of the same sex.

In adolescence, many transsexuals become acutely uncomfortable with their bodies. The development of secondary sex characteristics such as breasts and beards can be experienced as a betrayal of their inner identity and ends fantasies of becoming an adult of the hoped-for sex. Figuring out what their discomfort means, however, can be confusing, painful, and difficult. Some transsexuals find themselves romantically attracted to others of the same biological sex and may conclude that they are gay or lesbian. Some discover that dressing in the clothing of the other sex is pleasurable and wonder if they are *transvestites,* or *crossdressers*. For some, especially those who have been inculcated with conservative religious views or have had severely punitive parents, the idea that they might be deviant is so terrifying that they are unable to explore their feelings for many years.

Until recently, psychotherapists knew very little about transsexualism, and even now, most are given little or no training in this area. When a young man confides in a counselor that he is unsure of his identity as a man and has thought about changing sex, he may be advised to engage in more "masculine" activities and get married. Women who are uncomfortable with their sex may be told that they need a makeover or should have children. Unfortunately, these strategies do not work, only delaying the transsexual's discovery of his or her true nature and involving others in a difficult situation.

What causes transsexualism?

The cause or causes of transsexualism are currently unknown. Initial research suggested that factors in a child's early family experience might be related to the subsequent development of transsexualism. However, these factors are not found in the family histories of all transsexuals, and they are present in the childhood experiences of many people who do not turn out to be transsexual.

More recent research supports a biological theory of transsexualism. Many reports provide evidence for the theory that hormone fluctuations during gestation program the fetus's brain to develop a male identity or a female identity, or at least predispose it to accept later conditioning that solidifies gender identity. When this brain programming is at odds with the genitalia that develop, transsexualism results. Although evidence is mounting for this theory, it has not yet been proved.

It is also possible that some combination of biological and early childhood socialization factors produces transsexualism. Furthermore, the causes of transsexualism may not be the same for every individual. There is no evidence that transsexualism can be transmitted from one person to another or that a person can be convinced by someone else to become a transsexual.

Even though we cannot say for sure what causes transsexualism, we do know several things about it. Transsexualism appears to be established quite early in childhood. Most transsexuals say they have felt like a person of the other sex from as far back as they can remember, and often family members recall transgendered behavior in that person from an early age. Some children as young as three or four years of age state emphatically and persistently that they are "really" of the other sex.

We also know that *gender identity*, the conviction that one is of a particular sex, is not easily changed. Psychotherapy with teenagers and adults who have been diagnosed with gender identity disorder is uniformly unsuccessful in changing gender identity. Therapy with young children who exhibit transgender traits sometimes succeeds in changing children's outward behavior, but it is questionable whether gender identity has been altered. The long-term effects of this treatment are unknown.

How is transsexualism treated?

Consultation with a psychotherapist is the first step. If the client is unsure whether he or she is transsexual, the therapist helps the client resolve this uncertainty. Once this determination has been made, the therapist helps the transsexual decide on a course of action and the best timing for each step. Treatment generally consists of a gradual process of feminization for males and masculinization for females. Dressing in the clothes of their target sex and learning the culture and social skills of women or men are important parts of this process.

For transsexual women, treatment can include electrolysis to remove beard and body hair, administration of estrogens to produce more typically female body contours and breasts, surgery to convert male genitalia to a female configuration, breast implants, surgery to raise the pitch of the voice, and other cosmetic surgery. Transsexual men can have testosterone treatments, breast reduction, hysterectomy, and construction of male genitalia. The exact procedures that are undergone vary from one person to another, depending on the physical attributes they start with, their personal priorities, and financial constraints.

It is equally important for the transsexual to make changes in his or her legal status and on important documents. Having documentation that is congruent with one's appearance facilitates many aspects of daily living, such as using credit cards, showing identification when cashing a check, or producing a driver's license when stopped while driving. Name and sex can be changed on a person's driver's license, birth certificate, passport, college transcripts, credit cards, and other documents. Having the outward appearance of one sex while carrying identification showing the other sex not only proves inconvenient and embarrassing, it can also be hazardous. Transgendered persons have been taunted, assaulted, and even murdered by people who feel threatened by gender difference. In addition, they are sometimes mistreated by police officers and may not receive timely medical care in an emergency.

What are the results of this treatment?

Follow-up studies of transsexuals after they have completed their physical transition find that almost all are glad they did it. Because there are limits to what cosmetic surgery can accomplish, and such characteristics as height cannot be changed, some transsexuals are not entirely pleased with every aspect of their appearance after transition. Although surgical techniques continue to improve, newly constructed genitalia, especially in female-to-male transsexuals, may not function optimally. Hormone administration in male-to-female transsexuals can reduce libido and diminish capacity for orgasm. In addition, most transsexuals experience the loss of some relationships with friends and family members. Some lose social groups and religious communities that will no longer tolerate them once their transsexual status is known. Many lose their marital or partner relationships and their children. Some find that they no longer have the privacy they once did because of public attention focused on their lives. Almost all have their financial resources drained, and some also lose jobs or housing.

Despite the many losses and disappointments experienced by most transsexuals, the vast majority do not regret transitioning. Most are happier people and have found an inner peace that previously eluded them. For some, long-term depression that resulted from denial and suppression of their real selves finally lifts. Some find that once they have resolved their gender issues, there are other problems that remain; they can now turn their attention to these matters.

After transition, are transsexuals just like other women and men?

In appearance, body movements and gestures, vocal tone, and personality, many transsexuals are indistinguishable from nontranssexual men and women. Others are not. For some transsexuals, it is important to blend in, or "pass," and be able to live their lives without others noticing that they are different in any way. These transsexuals must create a revised personal history that is congruent with their new sex. At the other extreme, there are those who enjoy raising questions or creating confusion in the minds of others. They may purposely transmit mixed gender signals or let people know they are transsexual, with the goal of challenging stereotypes and popular assumptions about gender. Many transsexuals are very open, or even proud, about their transsexual history. Most neither announce nor hide the fact that they are transsexual; other aspects of their lives are more important.

Transsexuals have a unique history, unlike that experienced by nontranssexual men and women. They have been part of both the male culture and the female culture, whether they felt like they really belonged or not. They have had to examine who they are in more depth than most people, and they have made life choices most nontranssexuals never even think about. Transsexuals have usually spent time analyzing gender and its influence on people's personalities, capabilities, and thought processes, as well as the meaning of gender on a societal level. They often participate in a transgender community that has its own viewpoints and values and feels a connection with transgendered people throughout history and in every culture. Because of these experiences, transgendered people bring a unique perspective to the workplace and other groups they participate in.

Wouldn't changing the way transsexuals think be easier than surgery?

Several types of psychotherapy have been tried with transsexuals, but none has been effective in changing their gender identity. Some religious groups have attempted to convert transsexuals to "normal" women and men, with little success. Gender identity is well established by age two or three years and seems to be unchangeable after that; it may well be fully entrenched even earlier. Therapists who deal with gender issues today recognize that attempting to change gender identity in all but the youngest children is futile, and time is spent instead helping those who may be transgendered determine who they really are, make choices about how to live their lives, and face the challenges that lie ahead.

Boys who play with dolls and other girls' toys, prefer girls as playmates, enjoy dressing up in girls' clothes, and take the part of mother or sister in fantasy play are thought to have a greater chance of later identifying as homosexual, transvestite, or transsexual. Likewise, it is supposed that girls who enjoy rough-and-tumble play, prefer boys as playmates, like to play with trucks and guns, and take the part of father or brother in fantasy play are more likely to identify as lesbians, female-to-male cross-dressers, or transsexual men.

Young children who exhibit such cross-gender behavior are sometimes subjected to behavioral therapy, which can succeed in modifying a child's choice of toys and playmates. These children learn that their desires to play in certain ways are shameful and must be hidden, but there is no evidence that their inclinations are actually changed. In children who are transgendered, the consequences could include damaged self-esteem, increased confusion about their gender, and delays in discovering who they are.

Adolescents who behave in ways considered inappropriate for their sex have been treated with aversion therapy, hormones, and shock treatment, but their gender identity has not been altered. Attempts have been made to change gender role behavior by forcing teenagers into conforming behavior patterns—for example, making a girl wear dresses and showing her how to apply makeup, or making a boy play football or taking him hunting. These strategies often produce the opposite of the intended effect: they increase aversion for conventional gender roles.

Many transsexuals have thought that forcing themselves into gender-conforming behavior would change their gender identity. Young men joined the armed services (with slogans such as "the Army will make a man of you") or got married in hopes that acting out a male role would make them feel like men. Women got married and had children, hoping that some instinct would be activated that would make them happy to be women. In these cases, gender identity was not changed, but much unhappiness resulted as transsexuals found themselves burdened with obligations that prevented them from making personal changes, and spouses and children had to deal with a truly miserable individual.

Many transsexuals have spent decades trying to ignore their feelings or change the way they think, without success. As their efforts and those of the best psychotherapists and psychiatrists show, it is almost impossible to change a person's gender identity. Time spent trying to do so results only in years of frustration and depression.

2 A Closer Look at Transsexualism

What is the difference between transsexuals and transvestites?

Transvestites, who generally prefer to be called crossdressers, enjoy wearing clothes usually worn only by the other sex, and often they like to present the complete appearance of the other sex. Crossdressing is done on a part-time basis, and in general crossdressers have no desire to alter their sex. Some male crossdressers take estrogens to produce breast development, but most want to retain their sexually functioning male genitalia. Most crossdressers are heterosexual men, many of them married. Often they are hard workers and have well-paying jobs. They may be very secretive about their crossdressing due to fear of losing friends, family, spouses, children, jobs, and respectability if they are found out. Some belong to support groups that provide safe environments where crossdressers can socialize; others crossdress exclusively in the privacy of their own homes. Most male cross-dressers have used crossdressing for erotic stimulation at some time in their lives. Some gay men also crossdress, but again, they are happy to be men and value their male genitalia, unlike male-to-female transsexuals.

Less is known about female crossdressers. There are few social organizations that cater specifically to them; many identify as butch (masculine) lesbians and belong to the lesbian community. Historically, many women have crossdressed on a more or less permanent basis in order to gain access to or perform certain jobs (for example, jazz musician Billy Tipton and Civil War physician Mary Walker), but in most cases it is not known whether these persons were transgendered in the sense of having a gender identity as a man, or merely crossdressed in order to achieve goals that were otherwise unattainable by women in a male-dominated culture. Female crossdressers differ from female-to-male transsexuals in that they identify as women and have no desire to have male genitalia.

Is my transsexual employee gay?

Surveys that have collected data on sexual orientation in postoperative transsexual women show that about one third identify as lesbians, about one third consider themselves straight, and another third are *bisexual* (that is, they may be attracted to either women or men). A small percentage are *asexual,* in other words, not erotically attracted to anyone. For most transsexuals, the kind of person they are attracted to does not change when they transition. If a transsexual woman is attracted to men before she begins her transition, she will very likely still be attracted to men after she has completed surgery. There are fewer studies on female-to-male transsexuals, but it is known that gay, straight, and bisexual transsexual men exist.

It is important to note that *sexual orientation* is independent of *gender identity*. A person who identifies as a man can be attracted to men, women, both, or neither, whether he is transsexual or not. A person who identifies as a woman can be attracted to men, women, both, or neither, whether she is transsexual or not. Your transsexual employee may be gay, straight, bisexual, or asexual—that is a separate (and private) issue.

Is my transsexual employee at a higher risk of AIDS than other workers?

Transsexuality itself does not confer any risk of contracting AIDS. The same risk factors apply to transsexuals as to other populations: sharing needles for drug use, having unprotected sex (heterosexual or homosexual), and coming into contact with infected body fluids, such as blood, semen, and vaginal secretions. Transsexual workers are no more likely to be HIV positive than any of your other employees.

Do transsexuals have physical abnormalities?

People who have genitals that are not clearly male or female, or who have qualities of both sexes, are called *intersex*. In most cases, they receive surgical treatment for these conditions when they are infants. This surgery is performed to alleviate the distress of the parents: it is seldom required for the child's well-being and may in fact be detrimental. Multiple surgeries may be performed, causing scarring, diminished sexual sensation, and emotional trauma, and limiting options for later self-determination of sex. Intersex adults are now coming forward to voice their anger at having been subject to these unnecessary operations. Intersex children who are allowed to grow up without intervention may elect to have genital surgery as adults. Because of their anatomic anomalies, they are not diagnosed as having gender identity disorder, even if they decide to live in the other gender role from the one in which they were raised. Transsexuals, by definition, do not have physical abnormalities of the genitalia or gonads.

Are transsexuals mentally ill?

Although transsexuals may be diagnosed with *gender identity disorder*, which is included in the categorization of mental disorders used by psychiatrists and other psychotherapists to diagnose their clients (known as the DSM), it is not a mental illness in the same sense that schizophrenia, depression, and phobias are. The essence of the diagnosis of gender identity disorder is the persistent desire to change one's sex. Although it may be accompanied by depression or substance abuse, often due to the difficulty of getting competent help and the discrimination faced by those who cross gender boundaries, these are not features of gender identity disorder.

Therapists who are familiar with gender issues are an integral part of the treatment of transsexuals because they are trained to evaluate their clients' reasons for wanting to change sex and the probability that their clients' quality of life will be improved after transition. This professional examination helps to prevent irreversible hormonal and surgical changes in persons who have only a transient desire to change their sex and may later experience regrets. These short-lived urges sometimes occur in crossdressers or gay men during very stressful times, or can be part of a delusional system in psychotic persons.

Have transsexuals been abused as children?

Often, parents who fear that their children may be homosexual try to redirect cross-gender behavior and interest their child in more "appropriate" activities. In some cases, however, boys who show any sign of femininity or state that they want to be girls are severely punished, verbally abused, beaten, raped, or otherwise physically and sexually abused by misguided parents or other adults, who may believe that such treatment will toughen boys up or make them abandon their feminine behavior. Adolescent boys who don't seem masculine enough have sometimes been injected with male hormones against their will.

In addition, unfeminine girls and insufficiently masculine boys are subject to teasing and abusive treatment from their siblings and peers. Some children who are thought by classmates to be gay or lesbian are regularly threatened or beaten up at school. In a culture that stresses the importance of masculinity for males, some boys and men feel that they must demonstrate their own masculinity by ridiculing, intimidating, or injuring those who fail to follow the prescribed behavior for their sex.

Children are often taught in church or at home that homosexuals and gender deviants are sinners and will be punished by God or that they are mentally ill, dangerous, unstable, and prone to alcoholism and suicide. A child who suspects that she or he might be gay or transgendered may be terrorized by these characterizations, which can in some cases amount to mental abuse.

Although many transsexuals were abused as children, there is no evidence that abuse contributed to their transsexualism. The vast majority of children who are abused do not turn out to be transsexual. It is also important to note that in no case has abusive treatment resulted in a change in gender identity; rather, it traumatizes the child and adds to his or her difficulties.

Is transsexualism like multiple personality?

Multiple personality (now called dissociative identity disorder) is a strategy for dealing with trauma that is usually developed by very young children and carried forward into adulthood. In this condition, parts of the self are split off and compartmentalized, each often lacking awareness of the other parts. Once this mechanism is established, it is not uncommon for dozens of such splits to take place.

In gender identity disorder, a secondary personality may be created in response not to trauma but to social prohibitions on gender-deviant behavior, a development that occurs somewhat later than the age at which multiple personality evolves. In the case of a male-to-female transsexual, one "personality" may be a repository for feminine traits whose expression is forbidden and the other a façade of traditionally masculine traits used in an effort to be accepted. When these two sides of the self have been kept separate for many years, it may be difficult to disentangle which is the real self and which parts have been adopted for show. Therapy can help transsexuals sort out these parts of the self, but this process is very different from the treatment undergone by people with dissociative identity disorder.

Are transsexuals sexual perverts?

Three categories of sexual disorders are identified in the diagnostic classification system used by psychiatrists. First are sexual dysfunctions such as pain during intercourse and premature ejaculation. Second are the paraphilias, or disorders of sexual desire, which include exhibitionism, pedophilia, sexual sadism, and other disorders in which sexual arousal is obtained through unusual channels, or "perverted." Third, in a category by itself, is gender identity disorder, which differs from the paraphilias in that it has to do with gender identity rather than with sexual arousal (who one is, rather than what turns one on).

Transvestic fetishism, or sexual arousal of heterosexual men in response to wearing women's clothing, is considered a paraphilia. It is diagnosable as a disorder, however, only when it causes significant distress or dysfunction in a person's life. Some male-to-female transsexuals may be diagnosed with transvestic fetishism until they and their therapists recognize that the problem is actually one of gender identity. Transsexuals are *not* sexual perverts.

Is the suicide rate very high among transsexuals?

There are no accurate statistics on suicide rates among transsexuals because no one knows how many transsexuals there are and there is no system for tracking the gender identity of people who kill themselves. The available research suggests that transsexuals are probably more likely to commit suicide than nontranssexuals, but the rates are still low—less than 0.1%, or one in 1000.

Many of the reported suicides are related to the difficulty of obtaining treatment, lack of support, discrimination, and societal rejection of transsexuals. Others are due to untreated conditions such as depression, which can coexist with transsexualism and must also be addressed.

Why aren't there many female-to-male transsexuals?

The first transsexuals to request the intervention of modern surgeons, and therefore to come to the attention of the medical community, were male-to-female transsexuals. Thus, most of the early medical literature on transsexuals focused on those changing from male to female. Constructing male genitalia on a person born female is a much more difficult procedure and was not attempted until decades later. Mastectomy and hysterectomy are done frequently for medical reasons, so a female requesting these operations would not attract as much attention as a male requesting castration, which is performed because of disease only rarely. Persons transitioning from female to male can achieve very good results by taking hormones without having surgery. These hormones can be obtained through nonmedical sources such as veterinary suppliers and the black market, making it possible for some females who wish to masculinize their bodies to bypass the medical system altogether. For these reasons, female-to-male transsexuals have not been as apparent to doctors as have male-to-female transsexuals.

Transsexual men also do not precipitate as much social concern. It is more acceptable in our culture for women to wear men's clothing than for men to put on dresses. In fact, most male attire has been appropriated as fashionable clothing for women, including suits, tailored shirts, and ties. Some features of women's clothing, like shoulder pads, make them look more masculine. These items enhance a woman's aura of authority and competence and are often worn in the corporate business world. On the other hand, for men to don dresses or breast padding detracts from their credibility and their status. In a culture where women are second-class citizens, it is understandable that women would want to emulate men, but scandalous that men would want to take on the appearance of women, much less become women. Most of the media attention, therefore, has been directed at transsexual women, and the popular image of a transsexual is almost always of someone transitioning from male to female.

As female-to-male transsexuals become more politically active, access medical care more frequently, and form social organizations, it is becoming apparent that there are roughly as many transsexual men as there are transsexual women. Estimates of the ratio of the former to the latter have gradually risen from about one to four a few decades ago to nearly one to one currently.

Do transsexuals change sex in order to fill desired social roles?

Historically, some women have lived as men in order to perform jobs or achieve goals that were off limits to women. Less often, men lived as women. Today in the United States, there are fewer barriers to social roles for men and women based on their sex, so there is less need for individuals who want to take on certain social roles to masquerade as the other sex or to change sex. In some countries, where women are still extensively barred from some occupations, transsexual surgery is permitted for women who want to go into male professions. In the United States, however, sex reassignment surgery is not considered appropriate for those who want to change sex only to have access to certain roles or jobs.

Many transsexuals keep the same profession after they transition, as well as maintaining other interests and hobbies. Some give up certain leisure-time activities, such as building model railroads or knitting, only because they think such pastimes do not fit in with their new role; in this case, their new role restricts them as much as their old one.

Occasionally, people want to change sex in order to keep from being homosexual. A man, for example, who is attracted to other men might be more comfortable with the idea of changing sex and becoming a heterosexual woman than with the idea of being a gay man. This feeling is due to the extreme homophobia taught to many children in our culture. These homosexuals are discouraged from pursuing sex reassignment surgery, since their problem is not a gender identity at variance with their bodies but rather a self-hatred generated by a belief system that is incongruent with their feelings.

Is transsexualism a choice or not?

It is generally agreed that gender identity, the sense of oneself as a woman or man, is not chosen. It develops very early in life, as a result of biological or social events or both, and is unchangeable by the time adolescence is reached. Most experts believe that gender identity is fixed much earlier than that, and some hold that it is determined before birth and can never be changed. The amount of discomfort caused by having a gender identity that is mismatched with one's anatomy varies in different individuals from almost none to extreme anguish. The degree of discomfort experienced by a transgendered person is also thought not to be a choice. Although psychotherapy may modify this discomfort somewhat, it cannot by itself alleviate high levels of discomfort in transsexuals.

The decision to have sex reassignment surgery is a conscious choice based on many factors, including the degree of discomfort experienced by the individual, the responsibilities to which a person is committed (such as raising children), the probable effects on one's career, the limitations of available surgical procedures, religious beliefs, financial constraints, medical status, and more. It is a choice in the same sense that deciding to have a hip replacement is a choice: one would not do it just for fun—it is a course of action chosen because it alleviates pain and improves a person's quality of life.

3 Personal Histories

The following histories are not those of real people but have been drawn from the stories of many transsexuals to illustrate some typical elements in the histories of transsexuals who have transitioned while staying at their jobs. Because each individual is unique, a transsexual person's actual story may be quite different from the ones below. There is no "right" history for transsexuals and no single path through transition.

The following stories are examples of how transsexuals can successfully transition at work, but it should be noted that not all transitions occur smoothly. Some employees are victims of intolerant employers who fire them for being transsexual. Others may not know the best way to approach management and coworkers, resulting in misunderstanding and discomfort. Some begin transition without guidance from a therapist or support group, which can contribute to awkward timing—for example, too much breast development before adequate beard removal. Some transsexuals face constant harassment from coworkers or discrimination from management, which causes them to leave their jobs within a short time after transitioning. Many, however, report that they receive support and encouragement from both management and coworkers, and their transitions are accomplished with little difficulty.

Sharon, Formerly Steven

Sharon is a 42-year-old transsexual woman who has been working as a software engineer for 16 years. She is employed by a large software company that has had several transsexual employees over the last dozen years. She has been with her current employer for 11 years and has received very good performance evaluations. She gets along well with her coworkers, although she tends to be shy and keeps to herself.

Sharon began her life as Steven. As a child, Steven didn't like playing with the boys. They were too rough, and he didn't understand why they were so competitive. He preferred playing with his sisters or by himself. His parents saw Steven as an intelligent, sensitive child who seemed well adjusted. As he grew older, Steven felt that there was something different about himself—he wasn't like the other boys and had no interest in becoming more like them. He edited his high school newspaper and was well liked by his peers, especially the girls. He dated a few girls and found himself wishing he could participate in their social cliques. He couldn't visualize himself becoming a man and was dismayed by changes taking place in his body.

As a teenager, Steven tried on girls' clothing on several occasions and found it very pleasurable. It also scared him because he felt there must be something wrong with him. Although he told himself he wouldn't do it again, several times when he had the opportunity to put on women's clothing, he did. In college, he fell in love with a woman whom he later married, hoping that this relationship would put to rest his doubts about his masculinity. After a few years, however, he found that he still had an irresistible urge to put on women's clothing and to imagine himself as a woman. At his wife's suggestion, he went to a therapist who explained that Steven was probably a crossdresser and referred him to a support group for men who enjoyed wearing women's clothes.

After being reassured that crossdressing wasn't a mental illness, Steven started dressing as a woman once or twice a month and socializing with other crossdressers, sometimes bringing his wife along. However, the sense of being different was still there. Eventually, he returned to therapy and began a process of self-exploration that led to the realization that he wanted to be a woman—to be more exact, growing up he had always felt more like one of the girls, and now he had a deep conviction that he was, in fact, a woman despite his male body. After long discussions with his wife and his therapist, Steven decided to make the transition from male to female.

Sharon began electrolysis to remove her beard two years ago and began taking estrogen six months later. When her breast development started becoming apparent, she decided it was time to approach her employer. She told her manager that she was a transsexual and would like to begin coming to work as a woman a few weeks later. Since her manager had some questions about transsexualism, Sharon gave him some reading material. She explained how she had reached the decision to change her sex, and they discussed her plan for transitioning at work. Her manager said he would support her and asked her for the name of someone who could speak to her group of engineers about transsexualism.

Sharon then applied for a legal name change and obtained a driver's license with her new name and sex on it. She also changed her social security information. A week before she was to appear at work for the first time as a woman, her manager announced Sharon's plans to her coworkers, and a guest speaker explained transsexualism and answered questions.

On Sharon's first day dressed as a woman, her coworkers were curious, and all stopped by her cubicle on some pretense to have a look. Most were supportive but awkward in talking to her; one of the group of 18 engineers she worked with made a few offensive remarks and then generally steered clear of her. After a few weeks, things settled back into a routine, although it took several months for people to remember to call her Sharon and use feminine pronouns. Some still get it wrong.

Sharon's wife was unable to continue their relationship, so they divorced but remain friends. Their son, now 19, has moved away from home and doesn't want to see Sharon, although he will talk with her on the phone. Their daughter, now 17, lives with her mother and visits Sharon, but she doesn't want to be seen in public with her. Sharon is no longer welcome at her parents' house because they don't want the neighbors to see her, although her mother came to visit her once since she started living as a woman. One of Sharon's sisters is very accepting, but the other doesn't want Sharon to visit because she is afraid she'll have a bad influence on her children. The loss of family relationships has been very painful for Sharon, and she is hopeful that in time her family will accept her.

Sharon has been living and working as a woman for a year now and plans to have sex reassignment surgery in a few months. She says she is experiencing a sense of contentment that she never felt before, and she is excited about her upcoming surgery. Her coworkers say that, appearance aside, she has not changed much except for an improved sense of humor. Her manager is pleased with her continued good performance.

Loren, Formerly Heather

Loren is a 27-year-old police officer who transitioned from female to male two years ago. He has worked in the police department of a small Midwestern city for six years and has performed his job satisfactorily.

Loren grew up as Heather, a tomboy from early childhood. She climbed trees and played sports with the boys in the neighborhood. She was a sharp contrast to her younger sister who enjoyed playing house and dressing in frilly things. Her parents began to worry about Heather when she refused to wear dresses to school or church. They tried to interest her in dolls and jewelry, but she wanted nothing to do with them.

When Heather became a teenager, she played several sports in school and enjoyed looking so masculine that she was sometimes mistaken for a boy. She had several boys as friends but never dated them. As a sophomore in high school, she found herself very attracted to a female drama teacher, which inspired her to take part in theatrical productions. Once, when too few boys tried out for the school play, she was allowed to play the part of a man, which she found exhilarating.

The following year, Heather joined a gay and lesbian youth group and soon took an active part in organizing events. She made several new friends and began dating a girl from another school. Her parents were very upset when Heather announced that she was a lesbian, and they insisted that she see a counselor. After a few sessions, the counselor explained to Heather's parents that there was nothing mentally wrong with their daughter and suggested family counseling to help them understand lesbianism and communicate better with Heather.

By the time she left high school, Heather identified as a butch lesbian and a feminist. She had become politically active in the gay rights movement. After two years in college, she decided she wanted to pursue a career as a police officer. At the age of 21, she joined the police force of a small Midwestern city. She did well in the police department despite the fact that women were not always treated with the same respect or given the same opportunities as men. Heather learned to stand up for her rights here, too, which earned her a reputation of being aggressive and sometimes even abrasive.

Gradually, Heather began to realize that her masculinity went beyond that of other butch lesbians in her community. She learned quite a lot about transsexuals from a transgendered friend she met at a gay and lesbian political event. She joined a female-to-male discussion group on the Internet and spent a vacation at a conference where female-to-male issues were discussed. There she decided that she was interested in exploring sex change. When she got home, she had some difficulty locating a therapist who was knowledgeable about transsexualism and had to travel to another city to find one. After eight months of counseling, Heather decided to go ahead with transition; she chose the name Loren and began taking male hormones.

When Loren talked to the police department psychologist about his transsexualism, the psychologist offered to work out a plan of action with the police chief. At about the same time, Loren also confided in one of his friends at work, and soon rumors had spread throughout the department. Before the chief could issue a statement about Loren's plans, the media had learned that there was a transsexual in the police department. Confusion resulted, and it was several days before a statement from the police chief clarifying the situation and expressing support for Loren appeared in the press. Meanwhile, several people on the police force decided that Loren was an embarrassment to the department, and pressure was put on him to resign.

Loren agreed to a temporary transfer to a less visible position and had breast reduction surgery a month later. He then began living and working as a man. As he continued to take hormones, he grew a beard and his voice became deeper, making it easier for his coworkers to accept him as a man. After working as a man for a year, Loren had a hysterectomy but no genital reconstruction, since the cost was extremely high and he was not convinced that surgery would produce satisfactory results. He has no plans to have further surgery. He was transferred back to his former position after two years away from it.

Loren lives with a woman he began a relationship with several years earlier. She has decided to stay with him despite the change in their relationship, and now that he is legally a man, they are planning to get married. Loren's family accepts him, but they are uncomfortable talking about his transsexualism, so that subject isn't discussed when he visits them. Both Loren and his fiancée miss being part of the lesbian community, and their city is too small to have much of a transgender community. They have lost several friends, mostly lesbians, who don't call them anymore.

Two years after beginning his transition, Loren and his coworkers have adjusted to his change of sex. He gets along well with most of the other officers, and his job performance is satisfactory. He tries to ignore the occasional snide remarks he overhears. Loren feels he can concentrate better on his work now that his gender issues are resolved. He remains politically active, educating others about transsexualism and working for the rights of transgendered people. The local media has all but forgotten about him, although he has appeared twice on national talk shows.

4 The Process of Transition

Transition is the process of making the change from living as a man to living as a woman or vice versa. It is usually thought of as beginning when a person starts full-time cross-living and ending when genital surgery has been performed. These are, however, arbitrary beginning and end points. Before a male-to-female transsexual begins living full-time as a woman, she usually makes some changes in her physical appearance, such as piercing her ears, having a substantial amount of electrolysis to remove her facial hair, and beginning to take feminizing hormones. She has probably experimented with dressing as a woman for several years, both in private and in public. Female-to-male transsexuals may have mastectomies, begin taking masculinizing hormones, and practice dressing as men before actually living full-time as men.

Genital surgery, although an important step for many transsexuals, is seldom the end of transition. Electrolysis may continue, and cosmetic and voice surgeries may be performed, after genital surgery. Some transsexuals never have genital surgery but feel that they have finished transitioning once they have completed other procedures. For many transsexuals, becoming comfortable in their new role takes several months or years and has no definite end point.

What do psychotherapists do for transsexuals?

If a transsexual comes to a therapist without knowing what is distressing her or him, the first order of business is to identify the problem. A therapist who is knowledgeable in the field of sex and gender can be a helpful guide as the transsexual tries to understand her or his feelings. Making the diagnosis of gender identity disorder is an important step in the treatment of transsexuals because it makes them eligible to receive hormones and sex reassignment surgery.

The therapist does not attempt to cure the transsexual in the sense of changing his or her gender identity. Rather, the therapist acts as a teacher, transmitting information about what options are available, helping the transsexual sort out the pros and cons of each, and dispelling misinformation the transsexual may have picked up. The treatment for transsexuals is not a formulaic prescription, so the therapist cannot tell the transsexual what steps must be taken. Rather, choices must be made in the context of transsexuals' lives. Their relationships, families, careers, and financial situations must be taken into account. Timing is extremely important. Thus, the journey for each transsexual is as unique as that individual. It is the therapist's job to help the transsexual make decisions about what life changes to make, when, in what order, and how best to accomplish these milestones.

A good therapist should have access to medical and legal information and be able to refer the transsexual to providers of required services, as well as writing the letters of approval for these services. She or he should be able to advise the transsexual what to expect at each turn and how best to handle setbacks. If the transsexual decides to pursue transition, the therapist acts as a guide and advocate to help the transsexual through the series of steps involved.

Who decides when the steps of transition are taken?

Decisions about how to dress, when to have electrolysis, and whether to make minor modifications in physical appearance are made by the transsexual individual. When the transsexual begins to think seriously about taking hormones or having surgery, the first task is to find a knowledgeable therapist if he or she is not already seeing one. Professionals who treat transsexuals follow published *Standards of Care* that delineate protocols for ensuring that their clients are ready to take these steps.

In accordance with these guidelines, over a period of at least three months, the counselor determines whether the individual fits the diagnosis of gender identity disorder. When the diagnosis has been made and both the transsexual client and the therapist feel that the transsexual is ready for hormone treatment, the therapist refers the client to an endocrinologist or internist, who prescribes the proper hormones, monitors the individual for side effects, and adjusts the dosage as necessary. After the client has been living in her or his new gender for at least a year, genital surgery can be considered. Approval for this surgery requires the recommendations of two therapists, and the surgeon evaluates the transsexual client as well. Sex reassignment surgery is performed on most American transsexuals by several specialist surgeons in the United States, Canada, Thailand, and Europe.

Not all transsexuals submit to the procedures specified by the *Standards of Care*. Black market hormones are readily available, and sex reassignment surgery can be obtained in Mexico, Southeast Asia, and elsewhere without approval from therapists. However, individuals who bypass this process risk severe medical complications and tend to experience more difficulty adjusting to their new role.

What effect do hormone treatments have?

When female-to-male transsexuals begin to take androgens (testosterone), changes may begin to take place immediately and continue to intensify during the next few months. Although each individual reacts a little differently, some generalizations can be made. Facial hair growth is stimulated, and the transsexual grows a beard or must shave. Body hair also grows faster and thicker. Scalp hair, on the other hand, may thin, showing typical male-pattern baldness if this tendency has been inherited. The voice deepens and begins to sound more typically male. Changes may also occur in the skin; it becomes rougher and acne may develop. Body shape may change to become more like the average man's—fat is redistributed and it becomes easier to increase muscle mass with exercise. Menstruation gradually ceases, the clitoris increases in length, and the sex drive is heightened. Some transsexuals report increased feelings of aggression, dominance, ambition, and drive. It is not known whether these emotional changes are biological responses to testosterone or the result of expectations based on cultural patterns.

When a male-to-female transsexual begins to take estrogens, subtle changes become evident in two to four months. Again, individual responses vary, but generalizations can be made. Breast size increases and fat is redistributed in a more typically female pattern. Metabolism is decreased and weight is gained more easily. Muscle tone can be maintained through exercise, but it is more difficult, and some report a loss of strength. The skin tends to become thinner and more sensitive. Body hair grows more slowly and becomes thinner, but facial hair is reduced only rarely. Scalp hair becomes thicker and male-pattern baldness is halted, although significant regrowth is rare. The voice is not changed by estrogen treatment. The sex drive is decreased and the male genitals shrink. Some transsexuals taking estrogen report that their emotions are amplified, anxiety is decreased, and they experience a heightened sense of well-being. As in female-to-male transsexuals, it is unknown whether these are biological responses or are due to expectations based on cultural patterns, although transient depression has been documented when estrogen dosage is changed.

For both male-to-female and female-to-male transsexuals, there are several chemical forms of hormones available, several delivery systems, a range of possible dosages and timing, and the option of taking hormone blockers. Not everyone responds best to the same regimen, and several trials of different forms, dosages, and combinations may be necessary to ascertain the optimum regimen for an individual. These trials should, of course, be done under the supervision of a knowledgeable physician. Hormones can have serious side effects in some individuals, so close monitoring as hormones are begun is very important. A transsexual may require more frequent doctor's appointments during the few months when hormones are started.

After surgery, a maintenance dose of androgens for the female-to-male and estrogens for the male-to-female is established. These dosages are lower and serve to maintain the changes brought about by the initial hormone administration. Generally, the maintenance dose attempts to replicate the hormone levels found in healthy nontranssexual men and women. Once this stable regimen has been established, the hormones exert no noticeable effects.

For both male-to-female and female-to-male transsexuals, hormones help them develop the characteristics of the target sex to the degree that these are carried as potential traits in their genetic code. The amount of breast development transsexual women should expect can be gauged by the bust size of other women in their families. Transsexual men are likely to experience balding similar to other men in their families.

Some characteristics, such as bone structure, cannot be changed by hormones. Voices do not rise and beards are not lost when estrogens are taken or testes removed. Breasts do not disappear when testosterone is administered. Although the clitoris is enlarged when androgens are taken, it rarely becomes more than two or three inches in length, remaining smaller than the average male penis. When a male-to-female transsexual takes estrogen, the male genitals shrink but do not disappear, and no vagina is created. These limitations in the effects of hormones make some surgical procedures, as well as electrolysis and voice therapy, desirable for most transsexuals.

Fertility is lost by both male-to-female and female-to-male transsexuals. With our current state of knowledge, there is no way to enable transsexual men to produce sperm or allow transsexual women to carry children.

Most of the changes brought about by hormones become irreversible within a few months. After this time, stopping hormone administration will not result in complete reversion to one's original state. Thus, although the period during which hormones are taken is an important trial period for the transsexual to determine whether he or she feels increasing comfort with his or her body as it changes, it is also a concrete step in making the transition to the other sex.

What is electrolysis?

Permanent hair removal can be accomplished by *electrolysis,* a process in which each individual hair follicle is killed with an electrical current. It can be extremely painful, as a needle is inserted into the hair root and current applied through it. The amount of electrolysis needed depends on how much facial and body hair the transsexual has to begin with. On average, male-to-female transsexuals need about 120 hours of electrolysis for beard removal, which is usually done at the rate of a few hours per week.

Electrolysis may also be done on other parts of the body, to remove chest hair, for example. Thus, the whole process for transsexual women can take two years or more. Transsexual men may have electrolysis on the arm or genital area in preparation for some types of genital surgery.

For transsexual women, the most important area for hair removal is the face because it is so visible, but its visibility makes it difficult to accomplish electrolysis unnoticed. The hairs to be removed must be grown out for a day or two. After electrolysis, the skin is often inflamed for a few days, and there may be minor swelling and scabbiness as the area heals. Because of this timing, electrolysis is often scheduled on weekends so the transsexual's appearance at work doesn't attract attention.

What is cross-living?

Cross-living (sometimes referred to as just "living") is living full-time in the transsexual's new gender role. This means working or attending school, shopping, playing, relating to friends and family, going to church or temple, sleeping, and eating—doing everything in the new role. A period of a year or more of cross-living, called the *real-life experience* or *real-life test,* is required before surgery to give the transsexual a chance to experience what life will be like after surgery. Through cross-living, changing sex becomes more than a theoretical idea; the realities of life as a woman or as a man cannot be ignored. The transsexual is then better equipped to make a final decision about whether to continue on this path. For some, a longer period of cross-living is undertaken, either because they don't feel ready to make a decision about surgery or because financial or other circumstances prevent them from having surgery. Although other people are sometimes made uncomfortable by the transsexual's lingering in this state, it is better for transsexuals to take an extended period of time to make this decision than to be pushed to make a decision before they are ready.

What is involved in genital surgery?

The most common type of *vaginoplasty* (creation of a vagina) involves removing the testes and some of the tissue from the inside of the penis. In the most frequently used technique, the penis itself is inverted to make the vagina, and the scrotal tissue is fashioned into the labia. Skin grafting may be necessary if there is not enough penile skin to form the vagina. Some of the erectile tissue from the penis is usually used to form a clitoris, which can be responsive to stimulation if the nerve supply is left intact. Transsexual women have no uterus or ovaries, do not menstruate, and cannot become pregnant.

Phalloplasty, or construction of a penis for female-to-male transsexuals, is more difficult. Skin must be taken from another area of the body, usually the forearm or abdomen, to form the penis. Maintaining an adequate blood supply to the new organ is difficult, however, and not all such transplants are successful. A tube can be placed through the center of the new penis, allowing urination as in nontranssexual men. With newer techniques, the constructed penis may even be capable of sensation, but it cannot attain an erection.

Because of the high costs, which must almost always be borne by the transsexual, and the frequency of unsatisfactory results, many female-to-male transsexuals elect to have *metaidoioplasty,* a procedure in which the clitoris is freed from surrounding tissue so it can function more like a penis. No tissue is added to it, however, so it does not become any larger than hormone treatments have made it. This surgery is much less expensive than phalloplasty, the sensitivity of the organ remains intact, and the results are more reliable.

With either of these female-to-male procedures, the labia can be used to simulate scrotal tissue, which can be stretched to accommodate testicle-shaped implants. There is no sperm production in the transsexual man, so impregnating a woman is impossible. A hysterectomy may be performed to remove the uterus and ovaries, and the vagina may be surgically closed.

What other surgical procedures do transsexuals have done?

Breast surgery is common in both transsexual men and women. Most female-to-male transsexuals have breast reduction, or mastectomy, performed. In male-to-female transsexuals, hormone administration may produce adequate breast development, but often breast implants are desired.

Additional cosmetic surgery may be desirable, especially for male-to-female transsexuals. These procedures can include modification of the facial features to make them more feminine, hair implantation if male-pattern baldness has set in, and reduction of the Adam's apple if it is prominent. Cosmetic modifications may also be made to the genitalia.

5 More About Transition

How can transsexuals change their voices?

Some of the difference between male and female voices is due to the physical apparatus used to produce sound, and some is due to the different ways boys and girls learn to use their voices. The vocal cords in men are thicker than those in women and therefore produce a lower sound. In female-to-male transsexuals, androgens act on the vocal cords to thicken them, so the voice naturally drops. In male-to-female transsexuals, the vocal cords were thickened by testosterone at adolescence, and this effect cannot be reversed. Surgical techniques have been developed to increase the tension on the vocal cords, which prevents certain vibrations and eliminates the lower voice range. Unless the voice is retrained, however, the result can be a flat, somewhat monotone voice, which still does not sound particularly feminine. With or without voice surgery, voice training can help transsexual women to use their voices more like nontranssexual women do, and even to avoid the use of lower ranges. Transsexual men can likewise learn how to speak more like nontranssexual men.

How do transsexuals learn to act like someone of the other sex?

Young children learn how to act like girls and boys in part by watching the older children and adults in their environments, and teenagers look for role models to help them determine how to behave like women and men. In the same way, people of any age can learn more about the differences between women's and men's behavior by paying close attention, and with practice they can learn to change their behavior to more closely match that of other women or men. Because they identified with people of the other sex from an early age, some transsexuals picked up many of the behavior patterns characteristic of their target sex as children. For others, they are new. And many transsexuals are less concerned about conforming to societal norms for women or men than about simply being who they are. Just as nontranssexual women span the gamut from somewhat masculine to extremely feminine, so do transsexual women. Transsexual men can be just as masculine or as feminine as nontranssexual men.

Also of tremendous value are close friendships with members of the target sex. Becoming part of a group made up exclusively of men for the female-to-male transsexual or of women for the male-to-female transsexual can help enormously. These can be church groups, social groups, professional groups, support groups, or discussion groups. In these contexts, transsexuals can learn how members of their target sex relate to one another when they are by themselves.

How do transsexuals make legal changes of their name and sex?

In many states, a person can legally change her or his name merely by using the new name consistently (called the usage method). Legal name change can also be accomplished by filling out simple legal papers and going to court to request a name change. If a judge is satisfied that one's name is not being changed in order to defraud anyone, this request is generally granted. When a change is requested from a feminine name to a masculine one or vice versa, evidence that the petitioner is a transsexual under the care of a therapist and intends to have sex reassignment surgery is helpful.

Some federal agencies have clear, written policies for handling changes of name and sex, for example the passport authority. In other government agencies, there is no uniform policy and these matters are handled differently in each office. Results of requests for change of name and sex on documents may depend on the individual agency representative who is contacted. For some of these changes, a statement from a surgeon or therapist is required; for others, affidavits from people who have known the transsexual for a period of time are needed.

In some states, the Department of Motor Vehicles has a standard form for requesting a change of name and sex on one's driver's license. Some states issue new driver's licenses to preoperative transsexuals who provide documentation of their intent to change sex. Others require a doctor's statement that one sex predominates over the other or that sex reassignment surgery has been performed. After genital surgery has been completed, a new or amended birth certificate showing the transsexual's new name and sex will be issued by most states upon request.

Once a person has a new driver's license, Social Security card, or passport, it is fairly easy to get other documents, such as bank accounts, charge cards, and utility bills, changed. Many high schools and colleges will change the transsexual's name on transcripts upon written request by the transsexual. Former employers will often cooperate by changing the transsexual's records to reflect his or her new legal status.

How much do all these procedures cost?

Ongoing costs of transitioning include psychotherapy and hormones. Psychotherapy may begin well before transition and can extend indefinitely, depending on the individual's needs. Therapy can cost $300 to $500 per month.

Hormones are begun during transition and are usually continued for the rest of the transsexual's life. Estrogens for transsexual women and androgens for transsexual men cost $30 to over $100 per month. Anti-androgens, drugs that block the effect of male hormones produced by the body, are sometimes used by male-to-female transsexuals until the testes are removed. They range in price from about $50 to over $200 monthly. Alternative drugs are available for both female-to-male and male-to-female transsexuals who cannot tolerate those usually taken; they can cost up to $1500 per month.

For male-to-female transsexuals, electrolysis can be a major expense, depending on the amount of facial and body hair the transsexual starts with. Costs average about $8000 to $10,000. For those who began losing their hair before transitioning, hair transplants to cover bald spots can cost thousands more.

For female-to-male transsexuals, genital surgery costs range from about $10,000 to $15,000 for the simpler procedure and $70,000 to $90,000 for penile construction. Testicular implants may be an additional $3000. Transsexual men may have hysterectomies, which cost $10,000 to $15,000. Male-to-female sex reassignment surgery can cost from about $8000 to $30,000, depending on the surgeon. For both transsexual men and women, revisions may be required or cosmetic alterations desired, which can cost over $2000 each. Breast surgery, whether implantation or mastectomy, costs $6000 to $10,000. Voice surgery for male-to-female transsexuals costs $4000 to $5000. For all these surgical procedures, there may be additional costs for doctor's examinations and checkups, lab fees, hospital costs, prostheses, and travel to and from the clinics and hospitals where these procedures are performed.

Legal fees are a few hundred dollars in the simplest cases and can be much more if there is difficulty obtaining a divorce or custody of children. Clothing can be a major expense, because the transsexual needs to acquire a complete wardrobe, and may have to replace clothing because of changes in body contours during transition.

All in all, transsexuals who have added up their expenses estimate that they have spent $50,000 to $80,000 directly related to transition.

Will our company's medical insurance cover these procedures?

Most health insurance policies contain a clause specifically excluding sex reassignment surgery, even though it is a medically necessary procedure. At one time, this exclusion was justified because the procedure was experimental. Now, however, it has now been performed for over 40 years, has a documented record of success, and is the standard medical treatment for gender identity disorder. It is also much less expensive than many procedures that are routinely covered by health insurance (coronary artery bypass operations, for example). Insurers apparently continue to refuse coverage for sex reassignment surgery merely because they can, and this policy has not faced a court challenge in well over a decade. A notable exception to this tradition is Medicaid, which is legally bound not to refuse treatment on the basis of a particular diagnosis.

Insurance plans usually require transsexuals to sign a contract releasing insurers from covering any disorder related to sex reassignment surgery, even years after transition has been completed. Some exclusion clauses deny coverage for "all services related to sex transformation." This vague language allows insurers to refuse to pay for a wide range of services, including evaluation for gender identity disorder, hormones, physicians' office visits, hospital stays, operating room fees, and more.

Thus, although most insurance plans provide some coverage for psychotherapy, once the diagnosis of gender identity disorder is made, coverage for psychological testing, counseling, and other services may be denied. This is of particular concern to transsexuals because they are required to undergo extensive evaluation, to maintain contact with a therapist over a period of a year or more, and to obtain letters recommending surgery from two mental health professionals.

Hormone treatments may be covered by insurance if they are prescribed as hormone replacement or to correct a hormone imbalance, but if they are prescribed for gender identity disorder or transsexualism, they will probably not be covered.

Sex reassignment surgery for female-to-male transsexuals often includes bilateral mastectomy and total hysterectomy. These procedures are often done in non-transsexual women because of tissue or other pathology (for instance, cancer or endometriosis), so they may be covered if they can be shown to be necessary for these reasons. Other procedures, such as metaidoioplasty and penile construction, are rarely performed for reasons other than gender identity disorder and are almost never paid for by private insurers. The same is true for the castration and vaginal construction undergone by male-to-female transsexuals. As with any surgical procedure, there can be complications after sex reassignment surgery, and although these are usually minor and easily treated, they are seldom covered by insurance.

Breast implants, facial and genital cosmetic surgery, reduction of the Adam's apple, surgery to raise the voice, and hair implants to cover male-pattern baldness, are considered to be cosmetic, rather than medically necessary, surgeries and are therefore not covered by health insurance.

The language used in many insurer's exclusion clauses permits an overly broad interpretation. Because there is no standard for deciding what is related to "sex transformation," transsexuals sometimes have trouble getting insurance to pay for *unrelated,* medically necessary procedures. In one case, marriage counseling was not covered because one of the spouses was a transsexual. In another, an insurance company refused to pay for a mammogram to determine whether a breast lump in a transsexual woman was malignant or benign, even though they would reimburse for this procedure if it occurred in a nontranssexual woman (even if she were taking estrogens) or in a nontranssexual man. There was no evidence that the lump was related to sex reassignment surgery or hormone administration, but coverage was denied because of the contractual exclusion. In yet another case, a female-to-male transsexual was denied coverage for a hysterectomy needed because of very painful fibroids simply because he had been identified by the insurance company as a transsexual.

Some companies have made arrangements with their insurance carriers to provide coverage for their transsexual employees. These companies recognize that sex reassignment procedures are necessary for the health and well-being of their transsexual workers and that these employees will be better able to contribute in the workplace if they are not unduly burdened with the expenses of medical treatment. This is, after all, the rationale for providing health care benefits to all employees.

6 Work During Transition

How will transitioning affect my employee's productivity?

Before beginning transition, many transsexuals go through a period (decades in some cases) of confusion about themselves. During this time, transsexuals are vulnerable to depression; some even become suicidal. Often, they feel they can confide in no one, and they may not be fortunate enough to find a therapist who can shed light on their condition or a support group that can point them in the right direction. Suspecting that there is something abhorrent about oneself and hiding one's true identity from others can be extremely stressful. It is not surprising that employees in this situation may at times be distracted and unable to contribute fully at work. Some may even abuse alcohol or other drugs, further detracting from work performance.

Transition is a time of tremendous change on many levels. Obstacles, delays, and disappointments are often encountered. It is also a time of self-realization when the transsexual finally begins to shed the false persona he or she has for so long presented to the world and makes the changes that allow his or her inner and outer selves to become congruent. Thus the transition period is also a time of joy, excitement, and hope; many report a sense of peacefulness that has eluded them all their lives. While in transition, transsexuals are strongly motivated to earn enough money to pay for the desired procedures and to maintain above-average performance in order to keep their jobs; finding another job can be extremely difficult for a transsexual in transition.

Once transition is completed, a transsexual employee is likely to become more productive than before. Self-esteem has probably improved, the employee no longer has to hide who she or he is, and it is possible to concentrate more fully at work. The transsexual is now ready to settle comfortably into her role as a woman or his role as a man. Transsexuals themselves, as well as others in their environment, often report that after transition transsexuals are less irritable, more cheerful, and easier to get along with. It is likely that coworkers will discover the post-transition transsexual to be more relaxed and easier to collaborate with than before.

How much time off will my employee need?

Psychotherapy and doctors' appointments for monitoring hormone response will require a few hours monthly, either during or after working hours. Electrolysis is often done on weekends so the skin will have a chance to heal before the employee returns to work.

Some transsexuals like to take a few vacation days before beginning full-time cross-living to take care of paperwork and prepare themselves to appear in the other gender role. Some schedule their change in appearance to coincide with the end of a break such as summer vacation at a college. Others just choose a date and begin working in their new role without taking any time off.

The amount of time a transsexual employee needs to take off from work after having surgery depends on the individual, the type of work the transsexual performs, and the type of surgery. A hysterectomy is major surgery and requires a six- to eight-week recovery period, just as it would in a nontranssexual woman. Metaidoioplasty (freeing of the clitoris in transsexual men) and male-to-female genital surgery are less invasive procedures and may require a somewhat shorter recovery time. Minor surgeries, such as breast or testicular implants, usually require only one or two weeks for recovery.

After transition is completed, transsexual workers are no more likely than any other employee to need to take time off for medical or psychiatric problems. They are less likely to take maternity or paternity leave since their options for becoming parents are reduced.

Should my transsexual employee be transferred to a different location?

If transfer to a different location is a possibility, it should be discussed with the transsexual employee. A transfer should never be imposed on a transsexual worker without his or her consent, and such a move should not involve a demotion or a decrease in pay or status, or detract from the employee's career path.

There may be potential benefits for everyone, however, when a transfer is made on either a permanent or a temporary basis. It gives the transsexual's immediate coworkers time to adjust to the change of gender without the pressure of having to figure out how to interact with the transsexual on a daily basis. Coworkers who get to know the transsexual in her or his new gender role won't have as much trouble because they don't have a history of relating to the transsexual in the old gender role.

The transsexual may also benefit from a change of scene, because it is often easier for people to change their behavior when in the company of others who don't have expectations based on the past. On the other hand, a transitioning employee may prefer to remain with coworkers who are familiar, especially if they are supportive.

Should the transitioning individual's job responsibilities be changed?

Transsexuals both in transition and beyond retain their level of competence. In most cases, their job responsibilities do not have to be altered, although occasionally it may be desirable. Because transition is a time of great change for transsexuals, reducing the amount of stress they encounter at work can be extremely helpful. If the transsexual employee is in the public eye, temporary transfer to a less visible position may be desirable. If the transsexual worker deals with clients, she or he may prefer to be temporarily relieved of this responsibility or to change the specific clients she or he deals with.

While transsexual employees should in general be treated just like other employees, there are special situations that may arise. For instance, unless a transsexual woman has had voice training or voice surgery, she may be mistaken for a man on the telephone. If her voice might present a problem, for example in calling clients, she may prefer not to do this, at least for a while.

Each transitioning individual has different needs, and the possible benefits of changing job responsibilities should be weighed against the likely effects on the transsexual worker's long-range career goals. Each situation must be considered individually, with the transsexual worker's needs being evaluated in the context of the specific job environment and the company's goals. The transsexual employee should have a major input in these decisions.

How should my employee's contacts with the public be handled?

If your transsexual employee deals with the general public, for example as a sales representative, awkward moments might be anticipated. These situations could occur because your transsexual employee may present a somewhat ambiguous appearance as he or she begins to transition, or it could result from regular customers noticing a change in your employee. Judging from the experience of transsexuals who deal with the public, most customers are primarily interested in conducting business and do not seem to care much about gender changes in the person they do business with. If customers ask, however, it is best to have an answer prepared. A simple statement that your employee is a transsexual and will continue to perform his or her job as capably as before should be sufficient.

If it is possible to transfer your employee temporarily to a position in which she or he will have less contact with the public, it may be wise to do so. It is essential to discuss this idea with your transsexual employee to ensure that this transfer does not penalize her or him in any way. She or he may be eager to avoid awkward situations, or on the other hand may feel it is important to face these challenges head on. A solution should be agreed on that both you and your employee are comfortable with, and it should be made clear that the transfer is being effected to ease the transsexual's transition, not because she or he is an embarrassment to the company.

Transfers or changes in job responsibilities should never be made as a concession to actual or imagined narrow-mindedness on the part of coworkers, clients, or the general public.

Should my transsexual employee be restricted from working with children?

Children generally have an easier time accepting a transsexual's change of sex than adults do. Very young children have not been taught that sex doesn't change; they often believe that a boy could grow up to be a mother or that a person changes sex when they change the length of their hair. To these children, the idea that someone is changing their sex seems natural.

Children up to the age of six or seven are very attuned to gender cues and will notice gender ambiguity even when adults do not. It is no use telling children of this age that a transsexual woman is a woman just like nontranssexual women; they won't believe it. However, they are not necessarily judgmental. They have not yet been taught to hate people whose gender expression deviates from the two prescribed by our culture. After the age of about seven, when children have assimilated gender norms, they tend not to notice gender ambiguity as much as younger children.

The reactions of adolescents to transsexuals depend a great deal on how they have been raised. If their upbringing has emphasized rigid adherence to societal norms, they may have a hard time accepting gender difference. Teenagers may have assimilated the values of their parents; they may have learned to fear people who are different and to lash out at those who make them feel uncomfortable, or they may have learned to respect all kinds of people and to learn from those who are different. Among some groups of teenagers, gender nonconformity is accepted or even admired as a form of rebellion.

There is no reason that transsexuals should not work with children. Contact with transsexuals will not make children transsexual or gay or cause any mental disturbance. Transsexuals do not molest children any more frequently than nontranssexuals. Transsexualism is not a lifestyle that can be taught to children. Many transsexuals are fine parents and successful child psychologists, teachers, social workers, doctors, and others who work with children.

Parents may have reservations about their children having contact with a transsexual. This apprehension is largely due to ignorance about transsexualism and may be overcome through education if parents are open-minded. In situations such as schools, where many parents are involved, it may be possible to have a workshop about transsexualism for the parents. In other situations, difficulties have to be handled individually, and written materials or one-on-one conferences may be used.

Legal Matters

Are transsexual employees protected against discrimination by law?

Title VII of the Civil Rights Act of 1964 protects workers against discrimination based on race, color, religion, sex, or national origin. When transsexuals have filed claims that they have been discriminated against because of their sex, however, they have usually lost. Until recently, courts have held that the word "sex" in Title VII refers only to one's status as a man or status as a woman, not to a person's shift between these categories. This interpretation is beginning to change, and courts may be more inclined to protect transsexuals under Title VII in the future.

Because Title VII does not protect against discrimination based on sexual orientation, the Employment Nondiscrimination Act (ENDA), which would add sexual orientation to the list of protected categories, has been introduced in the US Congress. If passed, this act would protect gay, lesbian, and bisexual employees. Although this legislation has failed in the past, it is gaining support. Activists are working to ensure that the next version of this bill will specifically include gender identity as well as sexual orientation. If it does not, it is unlikely to provide significant protection from discrimination in employment practices for transsexuals because discrimination against them is usually based on their transgression of gender norms, which is not included in the definition of sexual orientation.

Some state, county, and city governments have enacted antidiscrimination statutes that include protection for transsexuals. Others have wording that might protect transsexuals, for example, prohibiting discrimination in employment based on medical history, genetic information, or personal appearance. In some states, civil rights acts prohibiting discrimination based on sex have been found to protect transsexuals. In many locales, test cases have not yet been brought, so it is uncertain how these statutes will be interpreted by courts. Eleven states, 10 counties, and 54 cities and towns had protections in place as of 2003, with the number growing each year.

In sum, there is no uniform protection. The outcome of court cases depends heavily on the specific jurisdictions where they are tried and the judges who hear them. Transsexual employees have been successful in lawsuits alleging discrimination in rare cases when laws protecting workers against discrimination based on sex have been broadly interpreted, when local statutes protecting against discrimination based on sexual orientation have been deemed to include transsexualism, and when local legislation has specifically included gender identity as a protected category. Religious organizations and the military are exempted from all regulations currently in place.

New legislation designed either to protect workers on the basis of gender identity (or gender expression or similar terms) or to exclude them from protection on that basis is being frequently introduced at federal, state, and city levels. Some legislation that would protect workers on the basis of sexual orientation specifically includes gender identity; some does not. The fate of these proposed laws is unpredictable; protections may be won and lost rapidly over the next several years. Overall, though, the clear trend is toward greater protection for transsexuals.

Many corporations and departments of government have outpaced the legal system and drafted their own nondiscrimination policies that include sexual orientation, and occasionally, gender identity. Now that more than half of Fortune 500 companies prohibit sexual orientation discrimination, companies in the forefront of the move toward greater workplace fairness are protecting their transgendered workers against discrimination. In 2003, twenty-one Fortune 500 companies, as well as many smaller companies, had such policies in place.

Is transsexualism considered a disability?

The Americans with Disabilities Act of 1990 provides protection against discrimination for workers with physical and mental conditions that substantially interfere with the performance of major life activities. An amendment to this act specifically excludes transsexualism from coverage, along with sexual behavior disorders such as transvestism, pedophilia, exhibitionism, and voyeurism. Although being a transsexual does not in and of itself interfere with the ability to perform almost any job, the biases and fears of others may do so. Transsexuals have usually been unsuccessful in court cases claiming disability status.

On the other hand, employees who have lost their jobs because of their transsexualism have sometimes made successful claims for receiving Social Security disability income. For example, a public high school teacher lost her job when her transsexualism was discovered by the principal and parents insisted that she be removed. Although she is still perfectly capable of teaching and she was well liked by students, she cannot get a teaching job. She now lives on disability payments. In this case, the transsexual is considered to have a condition that prevents her from working, even though it is actually not her disability but that of parents and administrators whose attitude precludes her employment.

Unlike the Federal ADA, state statutes may protect transsexual workers from being discriminated against because of their transsexualism. In these cases, an employer might be required to allow a transsexual employee to work as a member of the target sex, which is part of the prescribed treatment for this condition.

What are my legal obligations as an employer?

In areas where transsexuals are protected by law, employers must treat a transsexual employee like any other worker. Decisions regarding hiring, terms of employment, advancement, and termination must be based on the employee's performance, not on his or her status as a transsexual. In some locales, however, it may be legal to dismiss an employee for being transsexual, or to make other employment decisions on this basis. Even in these areas, though, if a transsexual worker who has been treated unfairly sues his or her employer, it is not certain how courts will rule. The safest practice is to treat transsexual workers fairly.

Courts have upheld an employer's right to specify different dress codes for women and men, as long as there is a reasonable justification for this difference. When some male-to-female transsexuals have started coming to work as women, however, they have been fired for wearing clothes that are too feminine; employers have tried to hold these employees to the dress code for men, resulting in lawsuits brought by transsexual women whose lawyers argue that employers do not have the right to specify their employees' gender. In other words, once a transsexual employee is legally a woman, she must be held to the same standards as other women. When a female-to-male transsexual legally becomes a man, he must be treated like other men.

Workers generally are entitled to a workplace that is free of intimidation, open hostility, or offensive behavior when this conduct is related to their race, color, religion, sex, or national origin. Even though transsexuals are not specifically protected by most antidiscrimination statutes, some courts have recognized that the intent of such legislation is to protect all workers from a hostile work environment. Increasingly, these statutes are being interpreted to provide protection to transsexuals. Employers would be wise to provide all their employees with an amicable work environment.

Although perhaps not required, it makes good business as well as legal sense to base employment decisions on workers' ability to do the job, to follow organizational guidelines for men and for women uniformly, and to ensure that no worker is impaired in the performance of her or his job by threats, harassment, or offensive remarks. These procedures permit transsexual and nontranssexual workers alike to be loyal and productive.

Is sexual harassment an issue?

Sexual harassment is behavior of a sexual nature that is unwanted by an employee, when (1) submission to such behavior is used as a basis for making employment decisions or (2) the conduct interferes with an employee's ability to perform his or her job or creates an intimidating, hostile, or offensive work environment. Since transition includes changes to the transsexual's breasts and genitalia, conversation about this topic may raise concerns about sexual harassment.

One way to prevent discussions that make the transsexual employee uncomfortable is to establish boundaries before an announcement about the transsexual is made to coworkers. Transsexuals vary in their willingness to talk about themselves and in their desire to educate others. The transsexual employee should be asked whether she or he wants to answer coworkers' questions or would prefer not to, and coworkers should be informed about these limits. Coworkers can be referred to other sources of information if they have questions that need to be answered. Helpful organizations, books, and videos are listed in the Resources section.

The transsexual employee should be advised that not all coworkers want to hear the details of transition, and their wishes should be respected. The transsexual should wait for coworkers to express their interest or ask whether they want to hear about his or her surgery, responses to hormone treatments, changes in sexual feelings, etc. before discussing these topics. Occasionally, a transsexual worker finds it hard to contain his or her enthusiasm about the changes he or she is experiencing and acts in a manner that could be construed as exhibitionistic or seductive. Such an employee should be told clearly that this behavior is inappropriate and, if the behavior continues, should be treated like any other worker who violates the rules.

Of course, unwelcome sexual advances, requests for sexual favors, and the use of sexually suggestive language are inappropriate when performed by or aimed at any worker, transsexual or not. However, the law prohibiting sexual harassment has been interpreted variously when transgendered employees are involved; if it can be shown that the behavior was based on gender identity rather than sex, the transsexual worker may not be legally protected. Nonetheless, it is in the employer's best interest to make sure that all employees follow guidelines for preventing sexual harassment.

How have other companies dealt with transitioning workers?

Hundreds of transsexuals have transitioned on their jobs, so many large companies and government agencies have had experience with these issues. Some have already had several transitioning employees. Because each workplace is different, the strategies that have been successful in one venue may not apply in another. A few generalizations may be made, however. Smooth transitions are marked by clear support from management, open communication between transsexual employees and company representatives, and insistence that transsexual employees be treated with respect. The greatest success is attained when management emphasizes the importance of teamwork, the positive value of a diverse workforce, and the need to accomplish assigned tasks. Difficulties have resulted when transsexuals have begun transitioning without discussing their situation with management, when employees have been discriminated against or fired for being transsexual, or when harassment and hostility toward transsexual workers have been permitted.

Occasionally, employers have thought that by firing a transsexual employee they could avoid negative publicity. If a lawsuit is filed, however, greater publicity can result and may reflect badly on the corporation or organization. Politically active transgender groups have organized in the past few years, and poor treatment of a transsexual employee is likely to draw negative attention in the form of letter-writing campaigns, protests, and demonstrations.

8 Support During Transition

What kinds of pressures does a transitioning individual face?

During transition, transsexuals must relearn many years' worth of gender-related behavior and figure out how to fit into a different gender culture. All the rules that young children are taught about what girls do and what boys do must be revisited. The knowledge that teenagers acquire about dressing and grooming, dating, and socializing with boys and with girls must be traded in for that of the other sex. The transsexual must become aware of the subtle differences in the ways men and women express themselves and relate to others of the same and the other sex. This gender re-education can be demanding and also anxiety-producing as transsexuals try out new social situations for the first time.

Relationships with others may be strained during transition. Family members may have a hard time dealing with changes in the transsexual's life and in some cases may sever ties with the transsexual. Likewise, friends may not be able to cope with transition and may stop calling. Transsexuals who are married or in relationships usually experience some difficulty. Not only is the transsexual person changing, but the nature of the relationship changes too. Although less frequently today than in the past, some therapists who approve, and surgeons who perform, sex reassignment surgery still require that married transsexuals obtain a divorce. This means that even if a transsexual and his or her partner want to maintain their relationship, they may have to get divorced nonetheless. For transsexuals with children, whether they are toddlers or adults, there are difficult issues to work out.

Transsexuals in transition may lose their social networks and spiritual communities. Often, transsexuals are held to be sinful and are no longer welcome in their church or temple. For transsexuals who formerly found support in lesbian and gay groups, transition may mean that they no longer belong in those groups. Those who are used to being part of the heterosexual world may need to learn how to interact in gay and lesbian social circles, where they may or may not be welcomed.

As mentioned earlier, there are financial pressures. Because most of the costs of transition are not covered by insurance, the transitioning transsexual must figure out how to pay about $50,000 for psychotherapy, hormones, surgery, and other procedures.

Many transsexuals, without legal protection or the resources to fight back, are fired from their jobs. Others put up with teasing, hostility, and discriminatory treatment in order to keep their jobs. One transsexual woman, not given permission to use either the men's room or the women's room, managed to refrain from using a restroom at work for the entire duration of her transition!

Will my transsexual employee receive support from her or his union?

In many cases, unions have been instrumental in obtaining fair treatment for gay and lesbian employees. Unions are often supportive of transsexual employees as they transition and can be helpful in ironing out difficulties with coworkers, conflicts with management, and problems involving discriminatory policies. In other cases, they may be unwilling to make much of an effort on the transsexual worker's behalf. Much depends on the individuals involved and their attitudes towards transsexualism, as well as the transsexual's prior relationship with her or his union. The AFL-CIO recently took an official position opposing discrimination against transgendered workers.

Will my transsexual employee receive support from the gay/lesbian/bisexual employees' group?

Gay/lesbian/bisexual groups do not automatically embrace transsexual members. They may feel that transsexual issues are so different from gay, lesbian, and bisexual issues that their group cannot address them. Transsexualism is not, after all, a sexual orientation, so some participants may feel that transsexuals do not belong in a gay/lesbian/bisexual group. Some transsexuals identify as straight, so they may question their right to attend gay/lesbian/bisexual meetings.

In recent years, many gay/lesbian/bisexual groups have been adding "transgender" to their titles and their mission statements. Some of these groups have been key advocates for transgendered workers. However, most members of these groups, like most heterosexuals, have had little or no experience with transsexual people. As these groups and individuals take steps to educate themselves about transsexualism, they become better able to provide the support transsexuals need.

How can management show support for the transsexual employee?

The simplest form of support is a statement acknowledging the transsexual employee's competence at his or her job and expressing the opinion that this competence will not change as a result of the employee's change of sex. Expressing the expectation that everyone involved will treat the transsexual employee with respect goes a long way toward effecting this attitude.

It is not enough, however, merely to *say* that the transsexual should be treated with respect. This attitude must be demonstrated by company leaders. Assistance should be provided to coworkers to help them understand the transsexual and spell out what is expected of them. Because relating to a transsexual is a situation that many people have never experienced, it is not always clear to coworkers what kinds of questions or suggestions might be offensive, how to properly address a person in transition, etc. It is crucial for management to follow through by taking swift action to correct any problems that arise in the workplace.

Employers can also be supportive by making it as easy as possible for the transsexual to attend regular therapy sessions, doctors' appointments, and support group meetings. Employers can help ease the financial burden on transsexuals by checking to see whether their insurance provider covers the required procedures, and if not, requesting that they begin this coverage or switching to an insurer that does. Company policies should be revised, if necessary, to include protection against discrimination on the basis of gender identity and expression.

Employers can encourage gay/lesbian/bisexual employee groups to provide support for transsexual employees by recommending transgendered speakers who can educate the group about transsexual issues and/or providing the resources necessary for this consciousness-raising to occur.

If your company makes donations to nonprofit agencies, consider making a donation to an organization that helps transgendered people. These national and local organizations provide invaluable guidance for transitioning workers and other transgendered people. Several such organizations, some of which are nonprofit, are listed in the Resources section of this book.

How do I know that changing sex is the right thing for my employee?

Transitioning from one sex to the other is not a process that is undertaken lightly. Your transsexual employee has probably spent many years in a process of self-discovery and thoroughly discussed her or his options with a psychotherapist. Most transsexuals are interested in making sure they don't follow a path that leads to increased misery. The focus of their work with a therapist is to make sure that they are making the right decision. If you have doubts about your employee's decision to change sex, contact a therapist who specializes in transsexualism. This person can explain the process and criteria therapists use in helping a transsexual make a decision about transitioning.

How can I be sure she or he is progressing satisfactorily?

It is a good idea for a manager to stay in close communication with the transsexual employee and his or her direct supervisor, either personally or through the human resources department. Each transsexual proceeds at his or her own rate and encounters different challenges, so each transition looks different. During the transition process, your employee remains in contact with his or her psychotherapist, who monitors the transsexual's development.

In rare cases, serious concerns may warrant asking your employee for permission to contact her or his therapist. The transsexual must also give the therapist written permission to discuss personal information with you or your representative. This contact is often best handled by a company psychologist, employee assistance professional, or the human resources department.

Remember that confidentiality is an important issue for transsexual employees. Because personal information about transsexuals fascinates many people, rules of confidentiality are sometimes broken and material that should remain in personnel files finds its way to other parts of the company, or even outside the company. When your transsexual employee entrusts you with personal information, whether directly or though a therapist, special precautions should be taken to safeguard this information.

How can I make my employee's transition as smooth as possible?

The single most important thing an employer can do is demonstrate support for the transsexual worker. This leadership helps to allay the fears of everyone who may be involved with the transsexual—coworkers, managers, clients, and the public—and provides them with a model for dealing with the situation in a rational, respectful way. A demonstration of support should be made as early as possible and should come directly from as high a level within the company as practical.

Another key component of a smooth transition is effective communication. The transsexual employee, as well as his or her coworkers and supervisor, should be encouraged to communicate frequently with a contact person in the human resources department or a management representative. Encouraging open communication is the best way to ensure that your transsexual employee is doing well, to discover any problems early enough to intervene before they become unmanageable, and to develop a plan that meets the needs of both the employee and the company.

For best results, the transition should be carefully planned. Anticipated problems should be discussed and strategies developed for dealing with them. A time line should be mapped out, with the understanding that dates are subject to revision. This planning should involve at least the transsexual worker and a management representative. The transsexual's psychotherapist, someone from the human resources department, a union representative, and/or an outside consultant might also be helpful.

Helping Others Adjust

How will the transsexual employee's coworkers react?

Most people are sympathetic toward transsexuals and believe they should be treated with respect and fairness. Without an understanding of what transsexualism is, however, some people react negatively based on misconceptions or on fear of the unknown. Almost all coworkers will feel awkward around the transsexual employee for a while. Because we all relate differently to men than we do to women, coworkers will feel a need to change the way they interact with the transsexual.

Sometimes people feel threatened by a person undergoing transition; those who have wanted to make various kinds of changes in their own lives—anything from losing weight to getting divorced—but lacked the courage or strength to do so may be resentful of someone like the transsexual, who actively creates her or his life. For some people, the actions the transsexual is taking seem immoral and they find it impossible to be supportive. Because the transsexual may plan to make changes in her or his genitalia, some people will feel embarrassed talking about transsexualism or just being around a transsexual. People may also feel uncomfortable because they don't know how to address the transsexual or they are afraid of slipping and using the wrong pronoun. They may be afraid of insulting the transsexual person by asking a stupid question or making a false assumption.

Often, people confide more in members of their own sex or say things they wouldn't say to someone of the other sex. Male coworkers may feel betrayed when one of their colleagues announces that she is "really" a woman, and female coworkers may be upset when someone they have related to as a woman says he is a man. What might they have told this person that they wouldn't say to someone of the other sex? How might they have treated the transsexual that would be inappropriate with someone of the other sex? In settings where rivalry is sensed between men and women, people may feel that the transsexual is "defecting" to the other camp.

While members of the transsexual's original sex may be quick to reject her or him, members of the target sex may be slow to embrace the transsexual. Female coworkers may not welcome the transsexual woman into their social groups, and male coworkers may have a hard time accepting the female-to-male transsexual as a man. If they have known the transsexual prior to transition, when she first presents herself as a woman or he first comes to work as a man, coworkers may not be convinced that this change is authentic. They may have trouble letting go of their previous image of the transsexual.

The example set by management is extremely important in determining how the transsexual worker is treated. If coworkers see managers treating the transsexual employee with respect, they are more likely to be accepting. If they receive a clear message that harassment will not be tolerated, even those who are uncomfortable will refrain from acting in a hostile manner. Once coworkers have had a little time to interact with the transsexual in his or her new role, they usually become more comfortable and can continue working with the transsexual as before. Many transsexual men and women who have transitioned on the job report that the great majority of their coworkers are not only tolerant but supportive.

How should my employee's transsexualism be announced to coworkers?

Such a statement can be made at a meeting called to announce the transsexual worker's intention to begin transition or it can be in the form of a memo. Management should express support for the transsexual employee, affirm its commitment to diversity in the workplace, and state the expectation that coworkers will cooperate to make the transition smooth. This announcement or memo should refer to the transsexual employee by the pronoun appropriate for her or his new gender role to demonstrate this usage to others. It can also be used to announce changes in restroom use, the appropriate person to refer questions to, and any meetings or training sessions that are planned to discuss transsexualism.

Many transsexual employees like to speak individually to at least some of their coworkers and immediate supervisors to let them know about their planned transition before a formal announcement is made. Others, particularly those with many coworkers, prefer to send a written message to the other employees explaining their transsexualism and their plans to transition, and expressing their hope that coworkers can be supportive. They may also take the opportunity to let others know a little of their history, what transitioning means to them, how they would like to be addressed, and that they understand how difficult it may be for others. This letter may be attached to the memo from management mentioned above.

How can I help coworkers adjust to this situation?

Most negative reactions on the part of coworkers stem from ignorance. One of the most helpful things an employer can do is provide coworkers with information about transsexualism and transition. The transsexual worker who feels comfortable sharing this type of personal information is an excellent source because the information is firsthand and applies to the transsexual in question. One limitation, however, is that many coworkers are reluctant to ask questions that they feel are too personal or potentially offensive. Another is that information provided by a coworker doesn't carry the weight that information coming from an "authority" like a therapist or doctor has.

Outside consultants or speakers can be very useful, including other transsexuals, psychotherapists or doctors who treat transsexuals, diversity training experts, or consultants who specialize in workplace transition issues.

Presentations can vary from lectures to panel discussions to intensive small group experiences. Depending on the number of coworkers, the type of interaction expected between coworkers, and other workplace variables, one or a combination of these resources may be used to advantage. See the Resources section for a list of organizations that can help you locate resources.

Written material can also be used to convey information to employees, but it should be followed up with at least the opportunity to ask questions of a knowledgeable person. This expert could be an outside consultant, a member of the human resources department, or a company psychologist. If company personnel are used, they should receive some training in the issues that arise in this special situation. Instruction in transgender issues is not part of most training programs for psychologists, human resources professionals, or diversity specialists. The best source for this information would be a psychotherapist or other professional who works with transsexuals.

What is the best timing for announcements, transfers, and other changes?

In most circumstances, coworkers should be told about a transsexual's plans to transition on the job two or three weeks before the transsexual actually comes to work in the new gender role. This timing gives them a chance to get used to the idea of the transsexual's new role before being confronted with the visual reality. The interim period is a good time to offer information about transsexualism to coworkers and/or to offer either voluntary or compulsory diversity training.

If the transsexual employee is to be transferred or have altered responsibilities, this change should take place at the same time he or she changes gender roles or very shortly afterward. In the event of a transfer, it may be wise to offer diversity training or other information to the new coworkers shortly before the transfer takes place. The transsexual could be introduced to his or her new coworkers at that time.

Many transsexuals who have transitioned successfully on their jobs report that there is a lot of curiosity during the first few weeks, that coworkers take a couple of months to adapt to the transsexual's new gender role, and that after several months they are accepted as members of their target sex without hesitation. If a temporary transfer is arranged for your transsexual employee, it should be tentatively planned to last for at least a year and perhaps two or three. It is important to maintain communication with your transitioning employee to determine the best timing for a transfer back to her or his original position.

Which restroom should my employee use?

Legally, a transsexual under the care of a psychotherapist is generally allowed to use the restroom appropriate for her or his current gender role whether or not genital surgery has been performed. Thus, once your transsexual employee has begun coming to work in the new role, she or he should use the restrooms designated for the new gender (women's rooms for male-to-female transsexuals and men's rooms for female-to-male transsexuals).

In the past some transsexuals have been forced to continue using the restrooms for their original sex even though they appear as members of their new sex. It is very awkward for everyone, however, when a man is present in the women's room or a woman walks into the men's room. Further, it violates the transsexual person's privacy by announcing to everyone in the vicinity (including visitors to the work site) that his or her genitals do not match the gender presentation, and in some cases it may expose the transsexual to a risk of violence.

Some companies have tried to use sex-reassignment surgery as the criterion for restroom use, but this approach is fraught with problems. For one thing, there is no single procedure universally recognized as sex-transformative surgery. During transition, the genitals may be transformed gradually by both hormones and surgeries over a period of time. It is difficult to know at what point the transsexual person's genitals are sufficiently altered to warrant a change in restroom use.

Further, many transsexual individuals never have genital surgery because of prohibitive costs, medical contraindications, or the risk of poor results. If restroom use is based on surgical status, such people would be required to use the restroom at odds with their gender presentation indefinitely. In addition, all new hires would have to be asked about their genitals in case one was a transsexual who had not had genital surgery.

Nontranssexual employees are not questioned about their genitals before they are given permission to use a particular restroom. If they were, cases would come to light in which a person's genitals might not sufficiently conform to the norm for either female or male, for example in intersex conditions, after accidents in which the genitals have been injured, or after treatment for genital disease.

In short, restroom use should not depend on genitalia. Since genitals are not used in the performance of most jobs, they should not be the subject of inquiry for employers or coworkers. Men and women are generally allowed to use the restroom consistent with their gender presentation without having to prove that their genitals conform to any standard, and transsexuals should be treated no differently.

On the other hand, other people in the workplace may not immediately feel comfortable sharing a restroom with a person they have known as a member of the other sex. Training can go a long way toward mitigating these feelings. When coworkers learn that their transsexual colleague is in the restroom only to do the same business as everyone else, they become more comfortable sharing a restroom with her or him. Coworkers should be reassured that the transsexual person is governed by the same regulations as everyone else. If the transsexual employee were observed engaging in any illicit activity in the restroom, the incident should be reported and would be dealt with just as it would if it involved any other employee.

Sometimes, inexpensive modifications to existing restrooms can resolve discomfort. Men's room stalls sometimes lack doors, and the barriers surrounding stalls in women's rooms are sometimes too short. Wide gaps in stall enclosures and doors that fail to lock or stay closed are common problems. Making sure the stalls in both men's and women's rooms provide adequate privacy helps everyone to share restrooms more comfortably.

In some companies, a temporary accommodation has been employed to give everyone time to get used to the change. For example, the transsexual employee may volunteer to use only certain restrooms appropriate for her or his new sex or only unisex restrooms for a month or two. The exact arrangement depends on the physical layout of the workplace and the radius of the transsexual person's work activities. After the specified period of time, the temporary arrangement ends and the transsexual employee is free to use any restroom appropriate for her or his new sex. By this time, most coworkers will have accepted the transsexual in the new role and will not give her or his restroom use a second thought. A coworker who continues to be distressed about sharing a restroom with a transsexual should be offered counseling.

In making arrangements for restroom use, it is important to recognize that neither the transsexual nor uncomfortable coworkers are at fault. They are both in a situation that challenges the assumptions of our gender system, and solutions are not ready-made. Every effort should be made to ensure that the transsexual employee has safe and easy access to a restroom. Usually, coworkers who are inconvenienced soon lose their discomfort with sharing the restroom with the transsexual employee.

How should my employee be addressed?

Usually, transsexuals choose a new first name that is more congruent with their new gender role. In situations where employees are addressed by their first names, the transsexual employee's chosen name should be used once he or she has started coming to work in the new gender role. When more formal terms of address are used, transsexual women should be called Ms., Miss, or Mrs., according to their preference, and transsexual men should be called Mr. Titles such as Dr., of course, do not change. Sometimes transsexuals change their last names as well as their first names. In this case, the new last name should be used as soon as the transsexual's gender role changes. Such name alterations are legal changes, very much like when a woman marries and takes her husband's last name, and paperwork changes should be handled accordingly.

Once an employee has changed gender roles in the workplace, pronouns appropriate to the new role should be used. A transsexual woman should be referred to with "she," "her," and "hers"; a transsexual man should be referred to with "he," "him," and "his." Because we usually use these pronouns automatically, it is difficult for most people to switch to using feminine pronouns for a person they have previously thought of as male, or vice versa. Even when careful attention is paid to pronoun usage, mistakes are bound to be made. For the transsexual, part of being accepted in her or his new role is being referred to by the correct pronoun. Most transsexuals understand how difficult changing pronoun usage is, however, and as long as a genuine effort is being made, they are not offended by an occasional mistake. The deliberate use of the wrong pronouns or use of terms like "it" or "he-she," on the other hand, must be considered malicious and dealt with accordingly.

Will my transsexual employee's behavior or appearance attract attention?

When male-to-female transgendered persons are portrayed in the media, they are often decked out in sequins, miniskirts, and way too much makeup. Female-to-male individuals may be costumed in black leather, with tattoos and chains. Most often, these are female impersonators, drag queens or kings, butch women, or crossdressers, but many people associate these images with transsexualism. Although there are some transsexuals who dress this way (just as there are some nontranssexuals who dress flamboyantly), there are many more whose dress is quite ordinary. Many transsexuals go through a period of experimentation with various styles of dress and grooming, just as teenagers do, before they find a style that works for them. Ultimately, they adopt the same range of casual, professional, and formal clothing that other women and men wear.

Of course, the workplace is not an appropriate venue for extreme forms of experimentation, and the same dress codes and rules for behavior apply to transsexual as to other employees. If you are concerned about the appearance your transsexual employee will present when he or she starts coming to work in the other gender role, ask for a picture of him or her in professional attire. If you still have concerns, these should be discussed with your transsexual employee. If he or she continues to dress or behave inappropriately, this issue should be dealt with the way it would with any other employee.

How should I handle uncomfortable clients?

Most often, clients are interested in the services they are receiving and are not concerned with the personal lives of the providers of those services. Occasionally, however, a client is uncomfortable working with a transsexual representative. Management's expression of confidence in the employee may fail to reassure the client, and the company's policy of nondiscrimination on the basis of gender identity may not impress the client.

Every effort should be made to help the client adjust to this unfamiliar situation. If this fails, however, the client may have to be informed that he or she has no alternative if he or she wishes to do business with your organization. Exceptions may be made in cases where clients are usually permitted to choose the employee they work with. For example, clients seeking psychotherapy from a counseling center are often permitted to select a therapist based on the therapist's personal characteristics.

In thinking about how to handle this situation, it is helpful to review your company's policies. How would a client be handled who refused to work with a Jewish or black or female employee? A client's discomfort with a transsexual employee should be handled the same way. Dislike for transsexuals as a class of people stems from the same type of ignorance, fear, and prejudice as intolerance of other groups.

What about coworkers who have religious objections to transsexuals?

Occasionally, a coworker feels that by undertaking transition a transsexual is acting immorally or sinfully. These people are, of course, entitled to their beliefs. They should also understand that the transsexual employee is not asking them to approve of or endorse any lifestyle, choice, behavior, or action. Management is directing them to treat the transsexual employee with the same respect due any human being. Many religions preach tolerance toward people who are different. Even if unable to be supportive, religious employees would be directed by this doctrine to work peaceably alongside a transsexual worker and to treat her or him with civility.

Some religions, however, direct their followers not to tolerate those they perceive as sinners in their environment. Some preach that believers must act to procure the salvation of all whom they believe to be damned. In this case, an employee might find it difficult to let a transsexual exist in peace. The coworker should understand, however, that the workplace is not an appropriate venue for proselytizing. The transsexual is not asking coworkers to alter their beliefs. Likewise, they should not use the workplace to try to persuade the transsexual that their religious viewpoint is correct.

In extreme situations, employees who are too uncomfortable to work with a transsexual may request a transfer or even quit. Coworkers who harass a transsexual employee should be warned that they face possible legal charges, formal reprimand, or termination. Their openly hostile behavior also makes the company vulnerable to lawsuits.

Will my international clients be offended if a transsexual representative is assigned to work with them?

Transsexualism is a worldwide phenomenon. In many parts of the world, traditional cultures have provided a place in society for transgendered people, whether or not they have made any surgical modifications to their bodies. In some cases, including Native American cultures, transgendered people were not only accepted but revered. Sex reassignment surgery was performed in Europe long before it was done in America. It is now performed in Canada, Mexico, Australia, New Zealand, Thailand, China, Japan, India, and other countries, and is paid for by nationalized medicine in some. Transgender groups are active in many parts of the world. The European Community extends more legal protections to transsexuals than does the United States. There is no reason to presume that people from other parts of the world will react negatively to transsexual employees.

10 Management Issues

Why is my transsexual employee doing this to me?

Most transsexuals who transition on the job want to make the changes they feel they must and also keep their jobs. Their purpose is not to shock others or to disrupt the workplace. They are changing sex only because it is a necessary step in their personal development and is essential for their happiness and well-being. Motivations for remaining on the job while transitioning may be to continue performing work they enjoy and are good at, to meet the expenses of transition and other financial obligations, or both. In any case, transsexual workers benefit from remaining responsible, productive employees and by transitioning as smoothly as possible.

Most transsexuals realize how difficult their transition can be for others, and they are prepared to be flexible, to overlook honest mistakes, and even to inconvenience themselves in order to make the transition easier for coworkers. A line must be drawn, however, at hostility and discrimination. When these are present in the workplace and are not effectively addressed by management, transsexual employees often quit or are forced to take legal action.

Couldn't this transition be done elsewhere?

Although it would doubtless be more convenient for many people if the transsexual could take a leave of absence and return a changed person, that is not the best course of action for the transsexual. First, it is not practical for most people because of the cost of both the procedures involved in transitioning and being out of work for an extended period of time. Second, the experience of living an ordinary day-to-day life, including making a living, is a vital part of the real-life experience and helps the transsexual to know that she or he can survive in the new gender role.

It is also to the employer's advantage to keep a valued employee on the job and avoid the costs of recruiting and training a replacement. Although many people would rather not deal with the issues raised by transsexuals, these are important questions for all of us to consider. They give us the opportunity to understand ourselves in a new way and to learn about the part played by gender roles in our culture. While having transsexuals in our environment may challenge us, it also enriches us tremendously.

Why hasn't transitioning on the job been a problem in the past?

Until recently, transsexuals were advised to disappear from the lives they were leading in their initial gender role and to reappear elsewhere as a member of the other sex. It was assumed that after transition, transsexuals would want to blend in as members of their new sex and keep their transsexual history a secret. Severing ties with people who knew them before transition—including church and social groups, friends and partners, employers and coworkers—and establishing new relationships after transition would make it easier to pretend they were not transsexual. It was also thought that transsexuals should take on stereotypical roles associated with their target sex, including gender-appropriate jobs. Thus, male-to-female transsexual engineers were expected to find employment as secretaries, for example. In fact, many therapists would not grant permission for sex reassignment surgery unless such a change was made.

Several fallacies in this model of transition have become clear. First, isolation during transition is not a good idea. This is a time when transsexuals need the support of friends, partners, and church and social groups. Second, many transsexuals choose not to hide their past, but rather to take pride in their personal history and in being transsexual. They often seek to further acceptance of transsexualism by educating the public about it and become active members of a community of transgendered persons that can provide support to others and push for political recognition. Third, the idea that people are restricted from holding certain jobs by virtue of their sex has been replaced by less discriminatory hiring practices, so it is not necessary for transsexuals to prove that they can be productive members of their target sex by holding a stereotypically masculine or feminine job. Finally, it does not make sense to require that a transsexual change careers at the very moment when they most need financial stability and maximum earning power.

In the past decade or two, therefore, transsexuals have begun to transition without changing their employment. Some large companies have already had several transsexuals transition in the workplace. Transsexualism is fairly rare, however, so many smaller companies have had no experience with transitioning individuals.

Will my employee try to recruit others to become transsexual?

Although many transsexuals are enthusiastic about their own process of self-transformation, most are very cautious about advocating sex change for others. They know only too well how difficult this path can be, and while it is extremely rewarding for certain individuals, it would be disastrous for others. Transsexuals are generally supportive of others who discover themselves to be transsexual and decide that changing sex is the right course of action for them. However, they almost universally discourage anyone who has not gone through a thorough self-examination and careful decision-making process from taking any irreversible steps toward changing sex. In any event, there is no evidence to suggest that a nontranssexual can be converted to a transsexual by any amount of persuasion or coercion.

Will my transsexual employee seek publicity?

Some transsexuals are deeply committed to educating others about transsexualism, and they therefore offer to speak publicly about their experiences. Others enjoy the attention they may receive from local and national media. Many, however, prefer to maintain as much privacy as possible while going through transition and would prefer that people didn't know they were transsexuals.

If you have concerns about how your employee might interact with the media, the best course of action is to talk to him or her about it. If your company has rules about what employees may say to the press or how they may appear (in uniform, for example, or with a company logo), these should be reviewed with your transsexual employee as early as possible. Additional concerns should be discussed with the employee. As they transition, most transsexuals are primarily concerned with making sure each step of the transition process is firmly in place. Their agenda usually includes staying employed and maintaining a good relationship with coworkers and employers, so transsexual employees are inclined to comply with reasonable requests.

Will the media be involved?

During the past several decades, thousands of Americans have changed their sex. Transsexuals have been exhaustively interviewed on television talk shows, and transsexual characters have appeared in mainstream movies and television dramas. Currently, the simple fact of transitioning from one sex to the other is no longer of much interest to reporters.

If your transsexual employee holds a prominent position, is in a position of authority or responsibility, deals with children, or serves the public, however, the media may find her or his transition newsworthy. Transsexual police officers, firefighters, armed services members, pilots, teachers, and politicians, for example, have been the focus of newspaper and television reports. In situations where transsexuals have been open and employers have been supportive, media interest soon wanes and a normal work routine can be resumed. In cases where employers have tried to hide the fact that they have a transsexual employee or have fostered controversy by expressing doubts about the transsexual employee, media attention is more sustained and often sensational. Transsexuals who bring lawsuits against their employers after being harassed or discriminated against also gain the attention of the media, as well as that of transsexual activists and human rights organizations, usually to the detriment of a company's public image.

In one case, a transsexual woman who is a commercial airline pilot sued her employer, who had fired her because of her transsexualism. She attracted media attention when she returned to work after regaining her job in an out-of-court settlement. Reporters asked passengers about to board the transsexual pilot's plane how they felt about flying with a pilot who had changed her sex. Quipped one woman, "I wasn't aware they used that part of their bodies to fly the plane." Her remark underscores the fact that, for most jobs, a person's genitals are unrelated to their job performance—a fact the airline should have considered before firing her.

What should be said to reporters?

An employer should simply state the fact that the employee in question is a transsexual, has made a decision to change her or his sex, and will in the future be coming to work as a woman or as a man. The statement should make it clear that management fully supports the employee in making this transition and that no change in the employee's job performance is expected. If the employee is going to be transferred to a less sensitive position, that can also be stated, although it should be framed as an effort to make the transition easier for the transsexual and coworkers rather than to protect the public from any imagined threat. If a meeting is to be held to inform the public and answer questions about the employee's transition, the time and place should be announced. In some cases, the employer may want to make the first move and call a press conference; in other cases it is prudent to wait until a reporter asks for a statement.

11 Workplace Dilemmas

The scenarios presented in this chapter illustrate some of the questions that arise when employers have transsexual workers. They have been simplified for presentation here, but all have been adapted from actual situations. Real life is usually more complicated, however, and the advice given here may not be suitable for all situations. Nonetheless, these recommendations have proved sound for other employers.

I suspect that one of my employees is transsexual. Should I ask her?

Until your employee decides to change gender roles at work, her gender identity is a private matter. Unless her behavior is unsuitable for the workplace, an employer has no justification for asking this personal question. Furthermore, whether your employee is transsexual or not, she may find your query offensive. You can make sure she and other employees feel safe to disclose this type of information by making sure your company's nondiscrimination policy includes gender identity as well as sexual orientation, and posting it in a prominent place. A memo can also be sent to all employees announcing or reminding them of the policy and reaffirming the company's commitment to a diverse workplace in which all employees are valued.

My transsexual employee has been cross-living for two years and does not seem to be any closer to having sex reassignment surgery. What's going on?

Although the required period of cross-living is only one year, no one should be pressured into sex reassignment surgery. Your employee may be taking plenty of time to make absolutely certain that surgery is the right course of action for him or her before taking this irreversible step. Because sex reassignment surgery is expensive and is not usually covered by health insurance, your employee may be saving up enough money for the procedure. Some transsexuals decide against having genital surgery for various reasons: for some, living in the desired gender role is satisfying and altering the genitalia is of minor importance; others have medical contraindications for this surgery; financial obstacles may be insurmountable; or the results of surgery may be too uncertain. As long as your employee is performing the job effectively, there is no harm in extending the period of cross-living indefinitely.

I supervise a transsexual worker who has started coming to work as a woman, but she's not very convincing. Should I tell her that she makes a better man than a woman?

Your employee is dressing as a woman because it reflects her inner gender identity, not because she thinks she is better looking as a woman than as a man. Her task during transition is not to convince others that she should be a woman, but to experience living as a woman so she will be in a better position to decide whether to have sex reassignment surgery. Making the transition from one gender role to the other is somewhat like what teenagers go through as they become adults. There is often an awkward phase as physical changes take place and the subtleties of social roles are learned. Be patient with your employee as she goes through this phase, and remember that her gender identity is not for you to judge—it is something she feels inside and is doing her best to express.

My transsexual employee is being teased by his coworkers. How do I know when they've gone too far?

Your transsexual employee may be enjoying gentle teasing by well-meaning coworkers, or he may be putting up a brave front to hide his hurt. The only way to know is to ask him. This conversation should be held in private, and you should make it safe for him to talk openly by not repeating to others what he says to you. Alternatively, he could be encouraged to talk to an employee assistance professional or a contact in the human resources department. If teasing is bothering your transsexual employee, a memo can be sent to all his coworkers stating that he is to be treated with respect and that continued teasing will not be tolerated. If a general notice doesn't solve the problem, action will have to be taken that focuses on the specific individuals involved.

Some of my employees are having a difficult time accepting their transsexual coworker as a woman because her voice is quite deep. What can I do to help?

Unfortunately, the voice of a male-to-female transsexual does not become higher when female hormones are taken or when sex reassignment surgery is performed. Surgery can be done that eliminates the lower tones from the voice, but it is quite expensive and there are few reliable surgeons performing this operation. Voice training, which helps people modify the pitch, tone, and loudness of their voices, can be undertaken and is advisable for transsexual women who want a more feminine voice. Local gender organizations can help locate a qualified voice training specialist if there is one in your area. However, not all transsexual women want to modify their voices; some note that women's voices occupy a wide range and feel it is important not to make extreme alterations in their bodies in order to become stereotypical women. Before you offer advice, ask your transsexual employee whether she would like feedback about her voice and other aspects of her transition. In time, her coworkers will get used to her voice, even if it is deep.

My transsexual employee keeps appearing on national television. Is he trying to embarrass my department?

Most likely, your employee is trying to educate the general public about transsexualism. Transgender issues are very misunderstood, and it is only through transsexuals speaking publicly about their experience that ignorance can be overcome. Over time, the collective efforts of many transsexuals will improve conditions for all transsexuals in their workplaces, as well as in their families, churches, and social groups. Embarrassing your department is probably the furthest thing from your employee's mind, but if it is a concern, he can be asked not to mention his affiliation with your company when talking to the media. Having a transsexual employee need not be an embarrassment; many companies are proud of their diverse workforce and use it to advantage in public relations and marketing material.

One of the police officers I supervise is a male-to-female transsexual. Could the hormones she is taking cloud her judgment or cause mood swings that would affect her ability to do her job?

Taking female hormones does not interfere with a person's judgment. Your employee may experience slight changes in mood when her hormone dosage is altered; these are similar to shifts in mood experienced by nontranssexual women during their monthly cycle or when they become pregnant and are not cause for alarm. Many transsexuals hold jobs that demand accurate judgment, decisive action, intense concentration, and a high degree of responsibility. They are commercial airline pilots, firefighters, police officers, sheriff's deputies, and others we all rely on. Taking hormones has not interfered with their ability to perform their jobs.

I have a postoperative transsexual employee who still lists her former wife as her spouse so she can receive health insurance coverage. Is this legal?

If your employee was legally married to her wife before she had sex reassignment surgery and they have not gotten divorced, they are still married even though they are now both women. Most lawyers believe this contract is still a legal marriage despite new legislation defining marriage as a union of a man and a woman. The application of this federal and state legislation to the situation of a marriage contracted between a man and a woman that then became a same-sex marriage due to one partner's sex reassignment has not been tested in court. As far as is known, your employee can legally list her wife as her spouse for health insurance and other purposes.

A transsexual employee in my department is dressing provocatively and acting sexually inappropriate toward her coworkers. Why is she behaving this way?

Sometimes, transsexuals are so pleased with the changes that are taking place in their bodies that they find it hard not to share their excitement with others. For some, it is pleasurable to see how others respond to their new body shape. Of course, this desire is no excuse for acting inappropriately in the workplace. Not having had much experience appearing in the world as a woman, however, a transsexual woman who behaves this way may not realize how others are reacting to her clothing or her actions. She hasn't had much practice dressing for work as a woman and may be unsure what is expected of her.

It is also possible that your transsexual employee is behaving no differently than other workers, but her actions may be misinterpreted by coworkers or clients because of misconceptions or stereotypes they hold. If you have ascertained that your transsexual employee is in fact behaving inappropriately, she should be spoken to in private about her behavior. If the situation doesn't improve, she should be dealt with in the same way as any other employee who behaves in this manner.

My transsexual employee is taking hormones and plans to begin cross-living in a few months, but he is not seeing a therapist. Is this okay?

It is important for anyone taking sex hormones to be monitored by a qualified physician. Reputable doctors will not prescribe these hormones to a transsexual without the recommendation of a therapist who has known the transsexual for several months. In order to protect his health, your employee should have both a therapist and an endocrinologist or other physician who can supervise hormone treatment. If your employee plans to have sex reassignment surgery, he will have to have the approval of a therapist who has worked with him for at least a year, so it makes sense for him to start seeing a therapist now. The entire process of transition is likely to be smoother if transsexuals have therapists and support groups to guide them. Tell your transsexual employee that you would feel more comfortable supporting him in his transition on the job if he were seeing a psychotherapist.

One of my employees just told me he is a male-to-female transsexual and would like to transition on the job. What should I do?

Meet with your employee to discuss her plans. Find out when she would like to start working as a woman, how she would feel most comfortable letting other people in the company know about this change, and whether she wants any change in her job responsibilities or location. Form a team that includes the transsexual employee, a management representative, and a human resources professional. An outside consultant who is familiar with transition issues can be an extremely valuable addition to such a team. This team should anticipate problems that might arise, such as with clients or with restroom usage, and devise strategies to overcome them. The team should also work out a plan for your employee's transition and a timetable for the changes that will take place, although this schedule should remain flexible. Consider hiring a consultant who is trained in this area to provide information to coworkers, facilitate communication between management and the transsexual employee, assist in obtaining legal information, and work with uncomfortable clients, the public, and the media.

12

Other Transgendered Workers

If your company has more than a few dozen employees, you probably have at least one transgendered worker. Transsexuals who are transitioning on the job make up only a small percentage of transgendered workers, however. Many other individuals would include themselves in the broad umbrella category of transgendered. Although this book focuses on transitioning transsexuals because they tend to present the greatest challenges to management and coworkers, it would be incomplete without a mention of other types of transgendered workers.

Intersex Individuals

Although transsexualism is thought to have a biological basis, the anatomic differences between transsexuals and nontranssexuals that have been found so far are subtle: some areas of the brain in male-to-female transsexuals are closer to the size found in other women than to that found in men. These differences can be observed only through the use of sophisticated medical technology or in postmortem dissection of the brain.

Intersex conditions, on the other hand, are generally based on obvious or readily discovered anatomic discrepancies in organs of the reproductive system and/or secondary sex characteristics. In some instances, genitalia may have both male and female features. In other cases, both ovaries and testes may be present, or the external genitalia may not be consistent with internal reproductive organs. These conditions have also been called hermaphroditism.

When a child is born with ambiguous genitalia (not clearly male or clearly female), physicians declare a pediatric emergency. A decision is quickly made about whether the child should be raised as a boy or a girl. Surgery to make the genitals more typically male or typically female is performed as soon as possible. This operation is usually not necessary for the well-being of the child but is done for the comfort of the parents and physicians.

Not all children with ambiguous genitalia are identified by physicians at birth, however. Usually only a cursory glance is given to the genitals, so some intersex conditions are missed. Intersex children born at home may not be brought to the attention of doctors. These children may grow up without surgical intervention, and parents decide whether to raise them as girls or as boys. When they reach adulthood, they may decide to have surgery to make their genitalia more consistent with the gender role in which they were raised, or they may decide to transition to the other gender role, much as transsexuals do. Some persons with unaltered intersex conditions choose not to have genital surgery, preferring to keep their bodies in their original state.

Some intersex conditions are not noticed until puberty, when a girl grows a beard or a boy develops breasts or begins to menstruate. Others may be detected only when tests are done to determine the cause of infertility or to prove eligibility for athletic competition. The latter group includes conditions in which the pattern of sex chromosomes (usually XX for women and XY for men) is at variance with the genitalia. For example, people with XY chromosomes who are insensitive to testosterone develop external genitalia typical for women. They are assumed to be girls, are raised as girls, and are usually feminine and identify as women. They are often surprised to discover as adults that they have a male pattern of sex chromosomes.

Intersex conditions pose no problems for the performance of most jobs. Although growing up with an intersex condition can be difficult, those who have done so are most often physically and emotionally healthy, and many are talented artists, ministers, scientists, social workers, and other professionals.

Crossdressers

There are far more crossdressers than transsexuals; some place the estimate at one in ten for men (and much less for women). Therefore, even a small company may have a crossdressing worker.

The great majority of crossdressers are heterosexual men, and many are happily married. They have little in common with gay men and lesbians and are unlikely to belong to gay and lesbian employee resource groups. Like homosexuality, crossdressing itself is not considered to be a mental disorder. If the urge to crossdress is upsetting to the crossdresser or if his behavior is interfering with his relationships or effectiveness at work, however, consultation with a psychotherapist is appropriate.

Most crossdressers have been wearing some clothes typically worn only by the other sex from early childhood or adolescence. Over their lifetimes, their interest in crossdressing may wax and wane, and their reasons for doing it may vary. Rarely, however, does the urge to crossdress disappear. Most men who crossdress report that this activity relaxes them and eases their tension. Some feel that they have a feminine side, or persona, that must remain hidden most of the time; crossdressing allows them to express this more feminine side. Sometimes, crossdressing is related to sexual arousal and activity, which is almost invariably solitary or carried out with a consenting partner.

Most male crossdressers like to present the complete appearance of women. They wear makeup, wigs, and padding to resemble breasts, which allows many of them to "pass" as women in public. Some enjoy partial crossdressing—wearing articles of women's clothing under their regular men's clothing, or sleeping in a nightgown. Female crossdressers who dress fully as men are rare, perhaps because women have much more latitude in their dress than men do.

Although many crossdressers fantasize about being women, few of them make permanent changes in their bodies, such as having electrolysis or taking female hormones; fewer still have feminizing surgery. For the most part, crossdressers have a solid identity as men, which would disqualify them as candidates for sex reassignment surgery. It is not uncommon, though, for transsexuals, particularly male-to-female, to identify as crossdressers for a period of time during their self-exploration. Sooner or later, they realize that crossdressing alone does not alleviate their distress; they must make changes to their bodies and join the other sex on a permanent basis.

Many crossdressers belong to organizations that provide a safe space for them to gather, usually crossdressed, and socialize. Others crossdress only in their own homes. Some enjoy going out in public—eating at a restaurant or going shopping—with other crossdressers or with their wives. Some have kept their crossdressing a secret even from their spouses and crossdress only when out of town. Conventions for crossdressers are held throughout the country and provide the basis for a national network.

In most cases, an employer never knows that an employee is a crossdresser. When they are not engaged in crossdressing, male crossdressers appear much like other men, and most keep their work life separate from their crossdressing. Quite a few have attained a high degree of success in their professions, which range from the military to computer science to sales to academia.

Fear of losing their jobs if their crossdressing is discovered is an enormous stress for many crossdressers. Legal protection for crossdressers is virtually nonexistent, and they are almost never mentioned in company nondiscrimination policies. Rarely, crossdressers have risked coming out at work, and a very few have openly crossdressed on the job and received the support of coworkers, management, and clients. Employers who judge crossdressers solely on their ability to perform their jobs often find them to be exemplary workers.

Postoperative Transsexuals

It is entirely possible that you may have unknowingly employed a transsexual who has already completed his or her transition. Many transsexuals are indistinguishable from other men and women, and their résumés may not reveal anything out of the ordinary. Records at the schools they attended and at their previous places of employment may have been changed to reflect their new name and sex, as have their social security cards, driver's licenses, birth certificates, and other personal documents. Transsexuals may have learned to speak of themselves in gender-neutral terms, i.e., as having been a child rather than a boy or girl, as being a parent rather than a mother or father, and as having a spouse rather than a husband or wife.

On the other hand, you may have a transsexual employee who is open about having had sex reassignment surgery in the past, or you may interview a prospective employee who volunteers this information. (It is not advisable for you to inquire whether an applicant is transsexual because of concerns about possible discrimination.)

The knowledge that an applicant or an employee is a postoperative transsexual should not be a basis for making employment decisions about them. Still, some information about such a person may be inferred: First, they have had to go through many hours of psychotherapy and batteries of psychological tests to ensure that they are free of severe mental illness. Second, in order to successfully complete transition, they must be goal-oriented, resourceful, persistent, and have a good sense of humor. Many of the qualities needed to get through transition are the same ones employers look for in job applicants.

Transgenderists

Not all people who change gender roles conclude their transition with sex reassignment surgery. Many are content appearing and being accepted as members of the other sex, and there are some good reasons for not undergoing genital surgery. The expense of this procedure is prohibitive for some, and health insurance usually fails to cover it. A small percentage of those who have undergone male-to-female sex reassignment surgery have little or no sexual feeling afterward, and many transsexuals prefer not to risk losing their libido or orgasmic capacity. For a few individuals, there are medical circumstances that preclude their taking sex hormones or put them at high risk of complications if they elect to have surgery. For some, changing their genitalia to match their gender identity is simply not very important; other aspects of the self loom larger. Others prefer not to have surgery on ideological grounds: surgery may be seen as an unnecessary mutilation of the body, or living in a manner consistent with their gender identity while retaining their original genitalia may be valued for the powerful political statement it makes.

Some cross-gendered individuals who do not have surgery call themselves nonoperative transsexuals; others prefer the term *transgenderist*. Whatever their reasons for not having sex reassignment surgery, they present more of a challenge to the dual gender system than those who cross neatly from one sex to the other. There is, however, no single correct way to be transgendered. The choices made by transgenderists are as valid as those made by transsexuals and crossdressers. Most transgenderists live and work full time in their chosen gender role and have identification showing this to be their social gender. They are frequently stable and talented individuals, and their transgenderism should present no impediment to their employment.

Drag Queens, Androgynes, Gender Blenders

Apart from transsexuals and other transgendered people we have discussed so far, there are many others who consider themselves transgendered. *Androgynes* present a somewhat neutral appearance—not really feminine, but not masculine either. They feel most comfortable with unisex clothing and grooming—styles that could be worn by either women or men. *Gender blenders,* sometimes called gender benders, combine elements of feminine and masculine, so their appearance is often unsettling to observers who expect to see a person who is readily identifiable as either a woman or a man. This mixed feminine/masculine appearance is often assumed precisely to create such an effect. There are also *bigendered* people who feel equally at ease presenting themselves as men or as women and may live part of their lives in each gender role. Their gender identity is not strongly male or strongly female.

Drag queens are gay men who dress as women from time to time because they enjoy doing so. They may attend parties or go to gay nightclubs dressed in drag. There are also lesbian women who enjoy dressing as men and call themselves *drag kings. Female impersonators* are men who dress as women, often as particular well-known women such as Dionne Warwick or Barbra Streisand, and perform professionally. They may be straight, gay, or bisexual and may or may not crossdress at other times.

As an employer, you could have any of these kinds of transgendered people working for you. The way they choose to express themselves outside the workplace has little relevance to their work performance. Although they may or may not have any legal protection against discrimination based on their gender expression in any given jurisdiction, they should be judged solely on their ability to perform their job. Of course, they do not have the right to act or dress any way they want on the job. They must follow reasonable dress codes for one sex or the other and are subject to the same disciplinary measures as anyone else.

Resources

The gender, or transgender, community consists of support groups, newsletters, organizations that provide resources and referrals, political action groups, informal networks, social clubs, web sites, gender clinics, and conferences for the benefit of transgendered people (including transsexuals, crossdressers, transgenderists, intersex persons) and their partners and friends. These organizations and events are run primarily by transgendered people and are an invaluable source of information and support for transsexuals in every stage of self-actualization. Workplace difficulties are among the issues addressed by many organizations. Often, local groups can provide speakers or written information or answer specific questions regarding transsexualism. Because many people with first-hand knowledge of gender issues are involved, these organizations often have more reliable, complete, and current information than academic or medical sources. The national organizations listed below can assist with contacting local resources.

National Organizations

Center for Gender Sanity
Address: PO Box 30313, Bellingham, WA 98228
Phone: 360-398-2878
Email: director@gendersanity.com
Web: www.gendersanity.com
▼ *Consults with employers who have transsexual workers; provides transgender diversity training; helps resolve specific issues related to transition in the workplace.*

FTM International
Phone: 415-553-5987
Email: info@ftmi.org
Web: www.ftmi.org
▼ *Offers information and networking for female-to-male transvestites and transsexuals during and after transition; provides services for women who are exploring gender identity issues.*

Gender Education and Advocacy (GEA)
Web: www.gender.org
▼ *Nonprofit organization that provides educational materials on many aspects of transsexualism and other gender variance.*

Harry Benjamin International Gender Dysphoria Association
Web: www.hbigda.org
▼ *Provides opportunities for scientific interchange among professionals; develops and publishes Standards of Care for the treatment of gender identity disorders.*

Human Rights Campaign's Worknet
Web: www.hrc.org/worknet
▼ *Maintains a database of information on workplace policies and laws surrounding sexual orientation and gender identity.*

International Foundation for Gender Education (IFGE)
Address: PO Box 540229, Waltham, MA 02454-0229
Phone: 781-899-2212
Email: info@ifge.org
Web: www.ifge.org
▼ *Educational organization that addresses crossdressing and transgender issues, publishes a magazine, distributes books, and sponsors conferences.*

Intersex Society of North America (ISNA)
Address: 4500 Ninth Ave NE, Ste 300, Seattle, WA 98105
Phone: 206-633-6077
Email: info@isna.org
Web: www.isna.org
▼ *Provides peer support, education, and advocacy for intersexuals—individuals born with anatomy or physiology that differs from cultural ideals of male and female.*

Pride at Work, AFL-CIO
Address: 815 16th St #4020 NW, Washington, DC 20006
Phone: 202-637-5085
Email: paw@aflcio.org
Web: www.prideatwork.org
▼ *National labor organization that exists to provide a resource for lesbian/gay/bisexual/transgender labor.*

Renaissance Education Association
Address: 987 Old Eagle School Rd, Suite 719, Wayne, PA 19087
Phone: 610-975-9119
Email: info@ren.org
Web: www.ren.org
▼ *Sponsors support groups where individuals can find safe space to learn about transgender behavior; provides education to professionals and the general public.*

Transgender at Work (TAW)
Web: www.tgender.net/taw
▼ *A valuable site for employers, HR professionals, and transgendered employees that focuses on cooperation among everyone involved in a workplace transition.*

Transgender Law and Policy Institute
Web: www.transgenderlaw.org
Email: info@transgenderlaw.org
▼ *Nonprofit organization working on law and policy initiatives designed to advance transgender equality.*

BOSTON
See IFGE above

NEW YORK
Gender Identity Project, Lesbian & Gay Community Services Center
Address: 208 West 13th St, New York, NY 10011

Phone: 212-620-7310
Email: gip@gaycenter.org
Web: www.gaycenter.org/programs/mhss/gip.html
▼ *Provides support groups and meeting space for transgendered individuals, as well as gay, lesbian, and bisexual persons.*

PHILADELPHIA

See Renaissance above

WASHINGTON, DC

Transgender Educational Association of Greater Washington (TGEA)
Address: PO Box 16036, Arlington, VA 22215
Web: www.tgea.net
▼ *Provides a supportive environment and social opportunities for transgendered individuals; educates the public and professionals who deal with the transgender community.*

ST. LOUIS

St. Louis Gender Foundation
Address: PO Box 9433, St. Louis, MO 63117
Phone: 314-963-4658
Email: stlgf@netscape.net
Web: www.transgender.org/stlgf
▼ *A resource group for crossdressers, transgenderists, transsexuals, androgynous individuals, and those who care about them.*

CHICAGO

Chicago Gender Society
Address: PO Box 578005, Chicago, IL 60657
Phone: 708-863-7714
Web: www.transgender.org/tg/cgs/cgsmain.html

▼ *Provides social and educational opportunities, as well as peer support, for crossdressers, transsexuals, and their supporters.*

MINNEAPOLIS

Program in Human Sexuality, University of Minnesota Medical School

Address: 1300 South 2nd St, Suite 180, Minneapolis, MN 55454

Phone: 612-625-1500

Email: colem001@maroon.tc.umn.edu

Web: www.med.umn.edu/fp/phs/phsindex.htm

▼ *Provides evaluation and treatment for people who experience discomfort with their assigned sex; offers mental health services sensitive to the needs of transgender and transsexual individuals and their families.*

DENVER

Gender Identity Center of Colorado (GIC)

Address: 1401 Saulsbury St, Suite G-9, Lakewood, CO 80215

Phone: 303-202-6466

Email: info@gicofcolo.org

Web: www.gicofcolo.org

▼ *Provides support to people who crossdress, are transsexual, or who are experiencing gender identity confusion, and to their family and friends.*

LOS ANGELES

Los Angeles Gender Center

Phone: 310-475-8880

Email: staff@lagendercenter.com

Web: www.lagendercenter.com

▼ *Offers psychotherapy to individuals, their partners and*

families dealing with concerns related to gender identity, sexual orientation, and sexual dysfunction.

SAN FRANCISCO

Trans Gender San Francisco (TGSF)
Address: PO Box 426486, San Francisco, CA 94142-6486
Phone: 415-564-3246
Web: www.tgsf.org
▼ *Provides support services and social events for transgendered people and maintains a hotline and a speakers bureau.*

SEATTLE

Ingersoll Gender Center
Address: 1812 East Madison, Suite 106, Seattle, WA 98122
Phone: 206-329-6651
Email: ingersoll@ingersollcenter.org
Web: www.ingersollcenter.org
▼ *Provides referrals to counselors and offers support, education, advocacy, and publications for transsexual, transgendered and transvestite people, their families and significant others.*

Recommended Reading and Viewing

BOOKS

Body Alchemy: Transsexual Portraits. Loren Cameron. Cleis Press, 1996. $24.95 paperback.
▼ *Striking photographic portraits of female-to-male transsexuals, including the author.*

Confessions of a Gender Defender: A Psychologist's Reflections on Life Among the Transgendered. Randi Ettner. Chicago Spectrum Press, 1996. $14.95 paperback.

▼ *Vignettes from the notebook of a psychotherapist who treats transsexual clients.*

Cross Purposes: On Being Christian and Crossgendered. Vanessa S. Sullivan Press, 1996. $17.95 paperback.

▼ *An intelligent discussion of religious objections to transgender behavior.*

Dear Sir or Madam: The Autobiography of a Female-to-Male Transsexual. Mark Rees. Cassell, 1996. $16.95 paperback.

▼ *The story of a British transsexual man in his own words.*

FTM: Female to Male Transsexuals in Society. Holly Devor. Indiana University Press, 1997. $49.95, paperback or hardcover.

▼ *A comprehensive look at the development of female-to-male transsexuals, with sections on etiology and history.*

Gender Outlaw: On Men, Women and the Rest of Us. Kate Bornstein. Routledge, 1994. $13.00 paperback.

▼ *An insightful and witty look by a transsexual woman at gender boundaries, fluidity, and definition in lesbian and straight communities.*

Identity Management in Transsexualism: A Practical Guide to Managing Identity on Paper.

Dallas Denny. Creative Design Services, 1994. $15.00, paperback.
▼ *A concise guide to changing one's name, changing sex designation on documents, and handling such issues as insurance, estate planning, marriage and divorce.*

Mirrors: Portrait of a Lesbian Transsexual. Geri Nettick, Beth Elliot. Masquerade, 1996. $6.95 paperback.
▼ *A candid account of the life of a transsexual woman and her struggle for inclusion in the lesbian community.*

Sex Changes: The Politics of Transgenderism. Pat Califia. Cleis Press, 1997. $16.95 paperback.
▼ *A contemporary history of transsexuality using in-depth interviews with gender activists, transsexual men and women, and partners of transgendered people.*

She's Not There: A Life in Two Genders. Jennifer Finney Boylan. Broadway Books, 2003. $24.95 hardcover.
▼ *The story of a transsexual woman's journey and the evolution of her relationships with those around her.*

Transformations: Crossdressers and Those Who Love Them. Mariette Pathy Allen. EP Dutton, 1989. $19.95 hardcover.
▼ *An album of photographs of crossdressers accompanied by their stories and those of their loved ones.*

Trans Forming Families: Real Stories about Transgendered Loved Ones. Mary Boenke, ed. Walter Trook. $13.95 paperback.
▼ *Brief accounts by parents, grandparents, spouses, children and siblings of transgendered people.*

Transgender Care: Recommended Guidelines, Practical Information, and Personal Accounts. Gianna E. Israel and Donald E. Tarver II, MD. Temple University Press, 1997. $39.95 hardcover.
▼ *A new look at the standards for transgender care and the stereotypes on which they are based.*

Transgender Warriors: Making History from Joan of Arc to RuPaul. Leslie Feinberg. Beacon Press, 1996. $27.50 hardcover, $16.00 paperback.
▼ *A historical perspective on transgendered people in a wide range of centuries and cultures.*

Transsexual Workers: What Coworkers Need to Know. Janis Walworth. Center for Gender Sanity, 1999. $12.00 paperback.
▼ *Booklet of basic information for coworkers told in the context of a transsexual woman's personal story.*

Transsexuals: Candid Answers to Private Questions. Gerald Ramsey, PhD. Crossing Press, 1996. $24.95 hardcover.
▼ *Information about transsexualism presented in a question-and-answer format.*

True Selves: Understanding Transsexualism. Mildred Brown, PhD, and Chloe Ann Rounsley. Jossey-Bass, 1996. $24.95 hardcover.
▼ *An explanation of transsexualism in plain language for families, friends, coworkers and helping professionals.*

Wrapped in Blue: A Journey of Discovery. Donna Rose. Living Legacy Press, 2003. $18.95 paperback.

▼ *A transsexual woman's journey of self-discovery and the emotional, physical, and spiritual challenges she faces.*

MAGAZINES

Transgender Community News. Renaissance Transgender Association. Monthly, $45/year.
▼ *Columns on transgender issues, coverage of community events, and more.*

Transgender Tapestry. IFGE. Quarterly, $40/year.
▼ *Articles, advice, news from the gender community, personal ads, and a directory of gender organizations and services.*

VIDEOS

Changing Sexes: Female to Male. Discovery Communications, 2002. $19.95 (available from Discovery 800-889-9950).
▼ *Explains transsexualism and tells the stories of four female-to-male transsexuals.*

Changing Sexes: Male to Female. Discovery Communications, 2002. $19.95 (available from Discovery 800-889-9950).
▼ *Explains transsexualism and tells the stories of four male-to-female transsexuals.*

Is It a Boy or a Girl? Discovery Communications, 2000. $47.50 (available from www.isna.org).

▼ *An exploration of intersex issues, including personal stories of intersex people.*

Metamorphosis: Man into Woman. $39.95 (available from www.ifge.org).
▼ *A documentary that follows a transsexual woman through her two-year transition.*

No Dumb Questions. Melissa Regan. Epiphany Productions, 2001. $75.00 or $199.00 (available from www.newday.com/films as a sale or rental).
▼ *Delightful short that shows the reactions of children to a transsexual family member.*

You Don't Know Dick: Courageous Hearts of Transsexual Men. Bestor Cram and Candace Schermerhorn. Northern Lights Productions, 1996. $250.00 (available from ucmedia.berkeley.edu as a sale or rental).
▼ *An examination of the psychological issues involved in transitioning from female to male.*

Glossary

asexual: not sexually attracted to either men or women

bisexual: sexually attracted to both men and women (not necessarily at the same time)

crossdresser (CD): person who enjoys dressing in clothes considered appropriate only for the other sex

cross-living: living full time as a member of the other sex

drag queen: gay man who enjoys dressing as a woman

drag king: lesbian who enjoys dressing as a man

female impersonator (FI): man who dresses as a woman in his role as a performer

female-to-male (FTM or F2M): starting female and becoming male

gay: homosexual, especially referring to men

gender: gender identity, expression, and/or role

gender expression: behavior, including clothing, that communicates one's status as a man or as a woman

gender identity: person's inner sense of being a woman or a man

gender role: constellation of appearance, behavior, and ways of thinking and feeling that is considered appropriate for men or for women

heterosexual: sexually attracted to persons of the other sex

homosexual: sexually attracted to persons of the same sex

intersex: having physical characteristics of both female and male

lesbian: homosexual woman

male-to-female (MTF or M2F): starting male and becoming female

nonop: nonoperative transsexual; a transgenderist

postop: postoperative transsexual, i.e., one who has had sex reassignment surgery

preop: preoperative transsexual; a transsexual who has not yet had sex reassignment surgery

real-life experience or ***real-life test:*** period of cross-living required before sex reassignment surgery

sex: categorization as female or male based on anatomic features (usually genitalia) or other biological markers such as chromosomes

sex reassignment surgery (SRS): surgical transformation of the genital area from the appearance characteristic of one sex to that of the other sex; may also include breast reduction in transsexual men

target sex: the sex toward which an individual is transitioning

transgendered (TG): having the gender identity or gender expression of the other sex

transgenderist: person who lives full-time as a member of the other sex without intending to have surgery

transition: the process of changing from living as a member of one sex to living as a member of the other sex

transsexual (TS): person who has transitioned or desires to transition from one sex to the other, usually including some surgery

transsexual man: transsexual who is born female and becomes a man

transsexual woman: transsexual who is born male and becomes a woman

transvestite (TV): crossdresser; more often applied to men than to women

Index